"I Can't Explain It,"

she said in a quivering voice. "You wouldn't understand."

"Why do you say that?" he asked softly. "Because you know how much I want to hold you? We're only postponing the inevitable," he continued. "I will hold you, Victoria, and kiss you. You know that. And I'll make love to you because I want you so much it's breaking me. And it's hurting you, even if you lie and tell me it's not."

LINDA SHAW
is the mother of three children and enjoys her life in Keene, Texas, which she shares with her husband. When Linda isn't writing romantic novels, she's practicing or teaching the piano, violin, or viola.

Dear Reader,

Silhouette Special Editions are an exciting new line of contemporary romances from Silhouette Books. Special Editions are written specifically for our readers who want a story with heightened romantic tension.

Special Editions have all the elements you've enjoyed in Silhouette Romances and *more*. These stories concentrate on romance in a longer, more realistic and sophisticated way, and they feature greater sensual detail.

I hope you enjoy this book and all the wonderful romances from Silhouette. We welcome any suggestions or comments and invite you to write to us at the address below.

Karen Solem
Editor-in-Chief
Silhouette Books
P.O. Box 769
New York, N. Y. 10019

LINDA SHAW
All She Ever Wanted

Silhouette Special Edition
Published by Silhouette Books New York

America's Publisher of Contemporary Romance

Other Silhouette Books by Linda Shaw

December's Wine

SILHOUETTE BOOKS, a Simon & Schuster Division of
GULF & WESTERN CORPORATION
1230 Avenue of the Americas, New York, N.Y. 10020

All She Ever Wanted

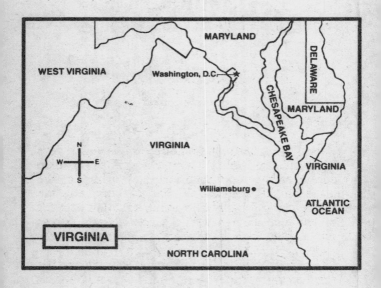

Chapter One

$\mathscr{I}$t was one of those glistening clear November days
that smelled of winter. Victoria Carroll stood ankle
deep in crimson and gold leaves, frowning at the
balance in her checkbook. For someone else the
figure would probably be a minor vexation. But for
her, a single woman with a school to run, it was
grim. *Depressing,* she thought with a shake of her
head, *utterly, utterly depressing!*

Kingspoint Bay lay considerably inland from the
Virginia coast. Fed by the Atlantic Ocean, it always
caught the backlash of seasonal winds. This year,
Victoria predicted, Brayntree School for Girls would
see a bitter winter, which was precisely why she had
just taken a delivery of three cords of chopped
firewood.

"You've gone up several dollars a rick on your
price, haven't you, Gordon?" she called as she
waded gracefully through the crunching leaves to-

ward a compact stone building, one of several which occupied the vast lawns surrounding Brayntree's ivy-encrusted main house.

Gordon Smith, a gangling youth of nineteen, walked to meet her. He tiredly mopped at his face in spite of the nip in the wind. He had just shoved the last split log into place and slammed the woodshed door shut.

"Had to, ma'am," he assured her in a gentle Virginia drawl. "This old truck don't realize the price of gasoline just keeps on climbin'.''

Grinning, he swept an experienced teenager's eye up from her finely-heeled leather boots, over the trim bias skirt, the classic pullover sweater and silk scarf to her short, copper-gilded waves. Her eyes were wide set and deep brown, not matching her hair at all. Her complexion just missed being that sensitive freckled coloring of a true redhead; it was quite fair and highlighted with pink, a creamy skin which would never take a tan and blushed with remarkable ease.

Though Victoria didn't consider herself beautiful, her features nonetheless fit together in a petite and intriguing fashion. She possessed a sparkling feminine appeal which caused men to stop and stare at her. Now, at twenty-two, she was almost accustomed to it.

She cleared her throat softly, distracting Gordon from his dreamy absorption.

"'Course," he added with quick embarrassment, "I could come down on my labor a tad if I had some help unloadin' it."

His clear eyes teasingly darted to the third floor of Brayntree's thirty-odd rooms, where nearly three dozen feminine eyes peered curiously down at both of them. Victoria followed the path of his fascination. As she tipped up her head most of her thirty-five students immediately—and prudently—withdrew their girlish faces to resume their afternoon art class.

She laughed. "It's much less complicated this way, Gordon," she assured him and signed her name to the check. She ripped it from the book and waved it at him. "Believe me."

Gordon released a deflated, wistful breath. "My mother says you get the finest girls in the state out here, Miss Carroll. Sure as heck the prettiest ones. You're goin' to keep the school open, aren't you? I mean since, well . . ."

"Since my mother died?" Victoria replied tactfully.

This was Victoria's first year managing Brayntree without Helen Carroll. Long before she could remember, Helen had established the exclusive girls finishing school, after she and John Carroll had divorced. Victoria could hardly recall the divorce. It had always been just the two of them.

Helen had taught her everything she knew and had adamantly insisted Victoria complete her master's degree in education, despite their chronic shortage of money. But she hadn't lived to see her daughter graduate. A year had passed now since she had buried Helen beside five preceding generations in the family cemetery at the back of the property. The passing of time without her had been emotionally draining, financially hazardous, lonely. She still missed her mother terribly.

Victoria drew on her habitually optimistic smile. "Brayntree's a tradition now, Gordon. Of course I'll keep it going." Her slender shoulders lifted in an uncertain, yet characteristically undaunted gesture. "I'll do what I always do—juggle bills against tuition, tell the cook to stretch the food more than is humanly possible and pray that something mechanical doesn't break down. Anyway, I appreciate your concern. Tell your mother hello for me. I'll try to see her on my next trip into Williamsburg."

As the three-quarter-ton truck made its way down the twisting slope of Brayntree's asphalt drive, its tires hissing on the damp pavement, Victoria lovingly peered about. From where she stood she could view almost the entire length of the peninsula jutting out into Kingspoint Bay, and the needle-thin glint of water in the distance.

Brayntree Estate's history, though not as impressive, was nearly as old as that of Virginia itself. The huge gray stone chateau had been built, not by an Englishman when King George ruled the colonies, but by a French nobleman who was rumored—since he left his wife and children on the Continent and never saw them again—to be in some difficulty with the French government. His architectural feat fit well into the narrow projection of land, like some precious jewel embedded in the sheath of an ancient sword.

Brayntree was a way of life to her now; she had never known any other. Since childhood she had planned to live out her days here as did her mother, and her mother before her, and her mother before that. Though she knew it was silly, she would blissfully hope for some fortuitous and totally impossible miracle that would keep her in the black until the end of the month. She would give her sixteen- to eighteen-year-old girls the finest instruction possible in academics, sports, the arts, proper grooming, fashion, sewing and the management of money. Then she would start all over again the next month.

Some yards away the heavily ornate east door

creaked open. Victoria obliquely caught the glimpse of girlish faces reappearing at the upper windows. Her assistant teacher and sometime secretary stepped from the shadows of the house.

"You're wanted on the telephone, Victoria," the older woman, whose grace Victoria had always thought remarkably resembled that of Deborah Kerr, announced. At times Stephanie Morris's efficiency bordered on the magical; she rarely met an emergency that she didn't know how to handle by some means. She was a godsend, though an underpaid one at present.

"Who is it?"

"I don't know," Stephanie answered back. "Some attorney who says his name is Pennington."

Except for Brian Levy, her mother's dottering old counselor who should have retired ten years ago, Victoria knew no other lawyer. Hurrying, her boots clicked emphatically down the hardwood length of the east corridor. She pushed open a door and stepped from the dark hallway into a large and gracious room whose tall windows captured the late afternoon sunlight. One entire end of the room, the one nearest a fireplace and a stairway to the upper floors, served as her office.

Smiling, leaning back against the edge of a massive Baroque desk and touching her throat with slender-tipped fingers, she lifted the telephone receiver and spoke into it.

"Miss Carroll?"

The masculine voice was vibrant with the leisured richness typical of Virginia-bred men. Yet, the drawl was laced with an educated precision she couldn't immediately identify. A northern university? Europe, perhaps?

"My name is Clifford Pennington of Pennington

and Associates," he continued smoothly. "A law firm in Williamsburg, in case you're not aware."

Victoria's pretty smile waned, then faded altogether. A gradual wariness intensified the brown in her eyes. "Go ahead," she said guardedly.

"My client is a Mr. Eliot Carroll. I have on my desk a petition by Mr. Carroll to procure his share of an inheritance from one Helen Carroll, his stepmother, *your* natural mother, I believe. According to my information, Helen Carroll's will has now been probated. Mr. Carroll, according to her last will and testament, is entitled to one half the value of a forty-acre property located at Kingspoint Bay and commonly known as ah . . . I have it here . . ."

Pages ruffled noisily from the other end of the line.

"Brayntree," she whispered dully.

It seemed to Victoria, as her eyes blurred out of focus, that she was experiencing *déjà vu*. With a vicious warning her memory envisioned herself listening on this very telephone when the hospital had called. *We are sorry to tell you that your mother passed away a few minutes ago,* they had told her.

Now she knew, with the instinct of a wild forest creature who smells the death of fire in the wind long before it can be seen, that this man's words could destroy her again.

"That is correct," he was saying. "It's imperative, Miss Carroll, that I make an appointment with you. I suppose you could bring certain affidavits to my office, but—"

"Wait a minute," she interrupted quietly.

"Of course, if you have the cash in hand you may be prepared to buy out my client's interest."

She felt as if she had been running hard; her

breath came in short, hard gasps. She groped for her chair. "Cash in hand?"

"Then I'm sure the most convenient thing would be for me to come there. That way—"

"Just-a-minute!" she cried shrilly.

Stephanie bent over her, gray eyes alarmed, scouring over Victoria's distraught features. "What's the matter, Victoria? Tell me."

Victoria hushed her with an uplifted hand. Swallowing convulsively and moistening her suddenly dry lips, she forcibly willed herself into a deceptive calm. "That is quite impossible, Mr. uh . . ."

"Pennington."

"Yes, well, Mr. Pennington, you see I've always known that Eliot was a beneficiary of Mother's will. Though he wasn't her natural son, she did love him and tried to be a good mother. But he hasn't lived here for nearly twenty years. Mother left a complicated will, and Eliot and I agreed, in order to not make things worse, that we would work out this property split between us."

"Miss Carroll, I'm sorry, but my client has obviously changed his mind. He has filed a formal petition."

"Damn the petition, Mr. Pennington! I don't care *what* Eliot has filed! He's never put one cent toward Brayntree. There's been a mistake, I tell you. Now, you get on the phone and call Austria, or wherever Eliot is now, and you tell him that I want this thing settled as we agreed at Mother's funeral."

The deep voice was inflexible and stern now, determined that she would not change things one iota. "Miss Carroll, you don't understand."

"It's *you* who doesn't understand!" She practically shrieked at Clifford Pennington.

"Victoria!" her frantic secretary hissed.

Covering the receiver with one palm, Victoria explained tonelessly, "Eliot has decided he wants his half of Brayntree immediately."

"Good lord! Just like that?" the other woman choked, as shocked as she.

Victoria felt the desperation of a mother about to lose one of her children. She was at her most dangerous now.

"I'm sorry, Mr. Pennington," she said coldly. "I'm afraid I can't possibly come to your office. And it's entirely out of the question for you to come here. Goodbye, sir."

Before she lowered the receiver she almost heard his teeth grinding. "Don't hang up, Miss Carroll," he flatly threatened her. "If you do, I'll have the deputy sheriff deliver a summons on your doorstep. I'm afraid that you really have no choice but to see me. We're dealing with the law here."

His words were quietly controlled, resonant with an authority as potently virile as it was legal. She decided, sight unseen, that she despised him.

"You know what you can do with your law, don't you?" she spat out the challenge. "I'm dealing with *justice,* not the law. They're two different things, you know."

"Becoming unreasonable won't enhance your position, madam," he retorted maddeningly.

She heard a harsh sound, as if he had angrily struck the edges of his papers against his desk. He went on. "I will arrive at Brayntree at precisely ten o'clock in the morning. And I'll bring a reputable realtor with me. The estate will be assessed as to its value and sold at a fair market price. You and Mr. Carroll will share equally in the proceeds."

"This is disgusting."

"I sympathize. Unfortunately, I have no choice but to abide by the laws of this state. Goodbye."

"W—Wait!" she sputtered and slumped forward to rest her chin on the limp heel of her hand as the line went dead. "That man is a . . ."

Stephanie's propriety was irreproachable, a legend, practically passed down from generation to generation. Yet now she stared down at the lifeless telephone receiver—they both stared at it—and she softly suggested, "The man is a bastard?"

In spite of the real horror of the last few minutes, Victoria gazed at Stephanie's perfectly serious expression. For once her secretary had no solution, and her uncommon crudity was, oddly, hilarious.

Victoria giggled, then sobered with a slow sigh. "Yes, that's exactly what he is. Stephanie, what in God's name will we do if Eliot can actually get away with this? Where do we go from here?"

A rustling from the doorway caused the two women to turn. Victoria counted at least a dozen heads craning around the facing, eyes dark with wondering concern, mouths pinched in anticipation of trouble. For all their maturity they looked like frightened little mice.

"Well!" she said with pretended energy, assuming the role she so often played when she wanted to tear her hair—the invincible bearer of all worries. "You might as well come in, girls. Chicken Little tells me the sky is threatening to fall."

One by one they filtered into the large room, finding their way without being told to, filling chairs and sofas, spreading over rugs and leaning against walls, as they exchanged anxious glances.

Automatically Victoria took up her pen and pad, walked to the front of her desk and retrieved a pair of wire framed glasses from her out-going mail tray.

As she fit them about her ears Stephanie moved behind the desk to jot notes and answer interruptions from the telephone.

"I suppose you all have major masterpieces from art class today?" Victoria gave them her most ironic expression.

"Roberta is a terrible model," someone giggled. "My sculpture looks like a Georgia peanut."

Someone groaned from the back of the room, "That's not really what it looks like, Miss Carroll."

Pressing back the treachery of tears, because she couldn't bear the thought of losing this, Victoria forced a smile. "Spare me, Betty. Anyway, I've known some rather nice Georgia peanuts in my time," she said and discreetly cleared her throat. Smiling again, more dazzlingly this time, she consulted a list of items from her pad. "Cathy, you, Doris and Sennica clear away the things in the art room. I don't believe there's any use trying to create any more art treasures today."

A pathetically faint trill of laughter rippled through the room. The suspicious minxes! she thought. They weren't buying any con jobs today. She frowned at her wristwatch. "At any rate, it's nearly time for dinner."

Doris Everman, an eighteen-year-old daughter of a state representative, drew herself up from off the back of a friend's chair. Unfortunately for Victoria, Doris had never been known for her tact.

"Something's happened, Miss Carroll. We deserve to know what it is."

"Yeah," several others agreed.

One girl raised her voice to be heard over the murmur. "You always said if we acted like adults, you would treat us like adults. What were you yelling about, Miss Carroll?"

"I wasn't yelling!" defended Victoria. Stalling for time then, something she didn't often do, she sighed, removed the glasses, looked at them as if trying to find a smudge and lowered them. "Well, perhaps a bit of yelling," she admitted.

Victoria met the sharp, accusing eyes of Betty Hallman. Her girls always went straight to the heart of things. It was her fault; she had taught them to do it.

"All right, Betty. Fair is fair. But I want you to understand from the outset, I don't believe anything will come of this that we really need to worry about. It's all a matter of bad communication. Annoying, but fixable."

"Is the school going to be closed down?" Sennica Ferris, with her usual drama, twirled out from the wall until she occupied center stage. "My father won't let me leave here, you know. He says that it's since I came to Brayntree that he's been able to walk through the jungle of my room."

"Mother'll up her tuition payments," another generous soul offered. "Since I clean up after myself in the bathroom she'll do anything."

"So will mine. I can cook better than she can."

They all laughed, and Victoria guessed she deserved a reward for looking out at all those sympathetic faces and not breaking down. Their respect had not been easily won; she had gone through hell with some of them, especially Doris Everman. Still, after a number of brilliant arguments, temper tantrums, demerits, rewards, hair-raising practical jokes and wonderful parties, they loved each other. She was certain that her heart was breaking!

Coughing, swallowing, Victoria attempted to steady her voice. "The school is not going to close down," she said hoarsely. Then she offered them the ultimate lie: "I promise. Cross my heart. Fight to the finish."

"Then what's the big deal?"

"One of the beneficiaries who holds an interest in this property," she explained, "is creating a slight tempest, that's all. But we'll get it settled. A lawyer is coming tomorrow to assess what we have here."

"If it's not a big deal, why'd you blow your cool?" one soft-spoken student asked.

"You're absolutely right, Dina," Victoria responded. "I guess I just didn't like the way the lawyer said it."

"Oh well, he's probably some old coot who doesn't know his head from his—"

"Doris," Victoria clipped, "You've got fifteen minutes to get the art room in order. I suggest you see to it now."

"I'd like to tell him a thing or two," Doris grumbled, heaving herself toward the door with a tromp of frayed jeans and tennis shoes and a toss of a wild, blond Afro. "Old goat probably wears false teeth and is scared spitless of women. I'd tell him to buzz off, in no uncertain terms."

Another chimed in, "He's probably the proud owner of one polyester leisure suit from a discount store who blinks and says 'Elvis *who?*'"

Victoria miscalculated when she thought she could unobtrusively blow her nose. As she reached behind herself for a tissue, hardly able to meet Stephanie's grim expression through the watering of her eyes, the room hushed as abruptly as if a film director thrust up both hands for immediate silence. The head mistress of Brayntree found herself blowing her nose in a startlingly loud manner.

"And I might add," she said quickly, realizing that

they saw through her as easily as crystal, "lest we have an epidemic of colds sweeping through here, check and see if you need an extra blanket from storage. If you do, see Bud before it gets dark. From now on the thermostat will remain religiously at sixty-eight degrees at night. I don't want anyone complaining that she froze." She put her pen and pad away. "I think we've about dissected Mr. Pennington's personal habits and preferences. Dinner will be in twenty minutes."

With the usual noises of intense suffering and complaining which drizzled out into the corridor, the girls soon cleared the office space. Victoria pressed her fingertips against her scalding eyelids and drooped with an enormous fatigue.

"You do that so well, Victoria," Stephanie complimented. Scooping up loose papers from the desk, she slipped them into a tray.

"How many times have we both watched Mother put on a show for the girls? You know, that woman should have been given an Oscar for the roles she played. Then, of course there was the last one, when none of us knew how sick she was."

Victoria's voice cracked like fragile aging tissue. Stephanie took several steps toward her superior and friend. Changing her mind, she wisely refrained from giving unwanted sympathy. If Victoria once let go she might crumble altogether.

"It's all right," Victoria said. Waving her away, she squared her shoulders with courageous resignation. "I understand Mother's purpose for making that stupid will like she did. But, my lands, Steph, couldn't she see what a mess she was leaving for me to cope with? I don't know what to do next. Try to talk to Eliot?"

"It wouldn't be a bad idea to wait and see what this Pennington fellow has to say tomorrow. Perhaps Eliot isn't the true culprit in all of this."

As Victoria jerked her head up her copper waves bounced silkily about her face. "You mean Daddy?" She pondered soberly. "No," she said, shaking her head. "I know he's generally broke, but he wouldn't talk Eliot into doing this."

Stephanie didn't look convinced. "Let's go eat."

Blowing her nose one more time, Victoria swept her arm out toward the door. "Perhaps things will look better on a full stomach."

The assistant teacher grimaced. "I know people say that, Victoria, but frankly, it never did much for me."

Victoria's laugh was sad and thin. "Me either. But it was the only cliché I could think of."

For the past year hardly a day had passed, especially during the school term, when Victoria hadn't taken her tour of Brayntree's kitchen. It wasn't that she didn't trust the judgment of her cook, Mamie Gardner, whose father's fame for his New Orleans cuisine reached even to Virginia, but Helen Carroll had never allowed a single detail of Brayntree to escape her. Now Victoria's same habit was deeply rooted in tradition.

Her inspection could easily be immediatly after breakfast when everything seethed with the confusion of clearing away and planning the day's nutrition. Or she had a habit—wearing a slim, belted robe and fuzzy slippers—of brewing tea in a dainty earthstone pot just before bedtime. As the chateau readied itself for slumber, she peacefully waited for the water to boil and snooped into almost everything without interruption.

"Come to sample the casserole, ma'am?" Mamie pleasantly invited as she threw back her wide shoulders. She wiped her hands with the glowing pride of an admiral at the helm.

"What? Oh yes, Mamie," she said. She remembered to congeal the smile on her face and thought, *If I don't find some way of getting around this Pennington man, some stranger will be overseeing this kitchen.*

She paused distractedly beside the huge oven and held out her palms to the radiant warmth.

"Potatoes with peas and diced carrots," Mamie reported. "Tiny green onions fresh from the winter garden and a rich gravy from yesterday's beef. Inexpensive to make and beautiful, just like you want it, Miss Victoria."

Victoria jerked her thoughts back to the cook's doubtful scrutiny. "Oh, yes. And with your heavenly crust, Mamie," she agreed, "it could easily grace the governor's table."

"The way you set table, ma'am, fried okra and cornbread could grace the governor's table. The Carroll women have always gone all out when it comes to meals. Good china and sterling and stemware at every place. Of course, I say that as a compliment, ma'am," she added hastily, lest Victoria think she was complaining.

Mamie wasn't exaggerating. Today's dinner would be served on heavy starched linen. The simple casserole, garnished with crisp parsley, would be accompanied with a fresh green salad and a delicate homemade dressing of real cheese. Jeans were traditionally forbidden at the evening meal. The girls would sit down with freshly-scrubbed faces and lively conversation. It would be an elegant, refined time, a time to heal up all the small and numerous difficulties of the day. And she was within a hair's breadth of losing it!

"I *say*, Miss Carroll!" Mamie was scowling. Victoria stupidly became aware of the fact that the woman was repeating what she had already said. "Do you wish to see tomorrow's menu?"

"Yes! Oh, I mean no, Mamie. I think not. And you will probably be at your own devices tomorrow. Get your weekly shopping list to me by Thursday, as usual."

Drawing her mouth, Mamie Gardner bestowed her a disapproving pucker.

Helen Carroll would never have done such a thing Victoria realized as she left hurriedly, without further comment. In the esteem of her dedicated cook her own stature—flawless until now—had just slipped a notch.

Unable to bear going into the dining room to sit and look at all the things she had worked so hard for, Victoria rushed to her suite of rooms on the far side of the chateau. They lay to the south and were not extravagant, but they were comfortable and tastefully furnished.

The large bedroom-sitting room was impressive with its inviting, uncluttered appearance. Carefully chosen antique pieces complemented the four-poster bed. A nicely appointed bath branching off one side balanced the private office on the other. Rich pecan paneling shut out the bustle of the outside world, but tonight silence was intolerable. She had to get out of this house!

She tore off her clothes and threw them toward a winged chair, not caring about the disorder. Yanking on a gray sweatsuit, she tied it securely about her tiny waist. Then she tugged on heavy socks and running shoes.

The riding path where she jogged was rarely used since Helen had died. Perhaps, Victoria wondered as she doggedly trudged past the stables, the wise thing would be to sell the remaining horses. The horses weren't all that valuable, but closing the stables would be the end of a tradition.

Her breath tore laboredly now, and she was soaked with perspiration. Who knew what was the best thing to do? Perhaps she should telephone old Brian Levy and file a counter petition. After all, Eliot and she had made a verbal agreement. Verbal agreements could still be binding.

Operating a place the size of Brayntree wasn't for a woman, anyway; everyone told her that constantly. Her banker thought she was a liberated lunatic trying to prove a point. He invariably dropped poorly-veiled hints about how long she intended to remain single. *Indefinitely*, she had told him with saccharine sweetness.

Every woman she knew who was her age was married and pregnant by now, or at least married and working. Was she going to be the typical "old maid school teacher"? Until this very moment that expression was the funny joke girls giggled about in junior high school when they griped about their homeroom teachers. Now it wasn't humorous.

She wasn't that different from other women. There were the same awful nights when she lay in her empty bed and would give anything to snuggle down in the arms of the man she loved and to hear him whisper, "I'll take care of everything, darling. Don't worry about a thing."

The truth was, men weren't exactly beating down her door to propose marriage. She and Brayntree were a frightening responsibility which sobered most men and made them think twice. The only man she had ever been remotely attracted to had finally, in desperation, delivered the ultimatum: him or Brayntree. She had told him there was no choice to be made.

Yet, if she were forced to sell Brayntree, what was left for her but to try to "find a husband"?

Slumping against one of the great gnarled mulberry trees a mile from the mainhouse, Victoria felt the heave of her own breasts, rising and falling, rising and falling. She placed her hands on them and crushed their virginal fullness, feeling the angry pounding of her pulse in her temples.

She was alone—completely, totally, horribly alone. Who cared that she needed someone or that she could never admit she was terrified of losing everything in a man's world?

When her head dropped wearily forward and almost touched her chest Victoria didn't wipe away the hot tears as they slid down her cheeks and spattered onto her sweatshirt to disappear. No one could hear her now. And she took some small, strange comfort in the soft wail of her own voice crying, "What am I going to do? Oh, God, what am I going to do?"

The three-storied main house of Brayntree Estate was built on a slope. Its foundation, though hewn and laid as any other stone foundation, was embedded in a natural footing of bedrock limestone thrusting out of the earth.

This sound architectural planning Victoria now found to be in her favor as she paced the floor at a quarter to ten the next morning. By stepping to any of the front office windows she could survey the hill's gentle incline which spilled westward in a narrow valley before it broadened out onto the main Virginia coastline. The entire length of the curving drive and its gates was visible to her.

Briefly, Stephanie stepped into the office for some notebooks. "I'll be glad when that man has come and gone," she said, truly annoyed. "Have you ever tried to analyze the Department of Interior when the students are sending grotesque signals to each other or staring out the window at the driveway?"

Running her fingers through her gleaming hair, Victoria remembered to smooth it back into place. She said, "Do the best you can, my dear friend. This shouldn't take very long. Then I think I'm going to place a call to Eliot, give him a piece of my mind and have a breakdown."

As the teacher adjusted her armful of items, unable to offer any comfort or encouragement, she tossed an impatient glance toward the windows, then paused, motionless. "I think your waiting is about ended."

Victoria flew to the window and distractedly chewed at her lower lip. A powerful, low-slung Porsche stopped at the open gates, then moved forward to purr slowly up the drive. For a moment she panicked, pressing both palms against her cheeks which were fiery with anxiety. Her eyes fluttered closed. Please, *please* make this work out somehow.

She shot Stephanie a look of perfectly wretched misery. "I need some fresh air," she breathed.

"Possession is still nine-tenths of the law," the other woman reminded her before she turned so Victoria couldn't read the doubt in her eyes. "Not exactly a piece of cake for this Pennington."

Victoria scooped up an overflowing file of pertinent papers: Brayntree's deed, a copy of her mother's will and several dozen accumulated receipts and assessments.

"A mouse is a fool to think it can win against an army tank," she muttered inaudibly. Whimpering a vague sympathy for herself, she stepped wearily toward the east door.

As Victoria walked toward a spacious graveled area which fanned out before a three-car garage, the brilliance of the sunshine blinded her. In spite of her nagging spirits she had taken meticulous care with her dress. She wore the same knee boots as before, because they were so finely made, and a simple, loosely-knit tube dress belted with a narrow leather cord. Her favorite Armani jacket topped it. Her only jewelry was a looped gold chain with an antique pendant which contained a miniature picture of her mother and herself. As the sun glinted into her hair it sparkled with at least three distinct shades of rust.

"Miss Carroll?" The short stout man who swung out the passenger side of the car was undoubtedly Clifford Pennington.

He was a typical lawyer, she noted with interest, viewing his thinning hair and scarred attaché and perfectly polished shoes. His thickened neck sprouted a jaw which wasn't nearly as formidable as she had expected. By the looks of him, his contrariness on the telephone was only a strategy to intimidate her. His ploy had almost worked, too—yet not quite.

Stepping forward, she held out her hand to meet the friendly one he proffered.

The taller man, the realtor whom she hardly looked at, appeared to be the exact opposite of his companion. She imagined him to be a super-aggressive salesman with his stylish sun-streaked brown hair and moustache. His pinstriped suit fit well. As he shut the door of the car she saw him fold a pair of sunglasses and slip them to an inside pocket. Trim-hipped and lean, attractive by anyone's standards, he was definitely a sophisticated man on the move and probably closed as many deals in the boudoirs of discreet, wealthy women as out.

Eager to have the ordeal done with now, Victoria riveted her attention upon the attorney.

"You're quite prompt, Mr. Pennington," she said with a courtesy which, though strained, was that of a gently-bred southern woman. "I trust this meeting will be brief. My time is valuable to me."

The man met her welcome with even more hesitancy than she offered it. An odd expression, a nonplussed angling of his brows toward the center of his forehead, made her blink. In that instant she interpreted what she saw correctly: indecision. She was certain that if she followed a basic law of nature—attack at the first sign of weakness in the opponent—she could place herself at an advantage.

"I'm prepared to counter your petition by my stepbrother, Mr. Pennington," she said officially, "on the grounds that he has violated a verbal agreement which I accepted in good faith. I am prepared to take it to court."

A deep voice interrupted from somewhere behind and above her head.

"A logical move, Miss Carroll," he drawled lazily. "But I'm afraid you have the wrong man. I am Clifford Pennington."

Chapter Two

Victoria made two unfortunate mistakes when Clifford shocked her with his announcement. The first was her miscalculation of how near he loomed behind her, since he stood barely two feet away. As she spun about, her wide, disbelieving eyes flicking to his soft brush of a moustache and an astonished "Oh!" shaping her lips into a dewy circle, her right elbow narrowly missed striking him in the chest.

Physical contact with a man she considered her enemy (by no stretch of the imagination was he her friend) was the last thing she wanted. In a badly-timed reflex she attempted to step back from him. The heel of her boot, however, twisted treacherously in the loose gravel. The papers which she clutched flew outward in a haphazard flutter of white and yellow and pink pages.

Her second mistake occurred when she finally

managed to regain her balance. With her wavy head tilted to one side, her eyes abruptly locked with those of the thirty-two-year-old man who unexpectedly bent over her. Fine lines webbed over the angular blades of his cheekbones. In the morning's light his irises were so richly hazel they were golden. For an isolated moment of time she stumbled into their amazing depths, completely unable to regain her composure or tear her own gaze away.

The breeze, meanwhile, scuttled her papers and blissfully sent them tumbling: deeds, tax receipts, insurance policies, surveys, wills and correspondence. She presently turned to view them scattered over the driveway and the lawn, mingling with fallen leaves beneath the trees.

"Oh, dear!" she exclaimed and bleakly lifted both her hands.

"Indeed," he agreed pleasantly and placed a foot upon a profit and loss statement as it whisked past his shoe.

When he proffered it she suffered such acute dismay she snatched it in a blaze of haughtiness. She was almost certain she heard him chuckle. Hotly embarrassed now, since not only had she mistaken who he was and ruined her bluff of a countersuit, she looked like a bumbling teenager.

She stepped quickly to retrieve what few papers she could. Clifford saw his stocky companion already moving past them to capture the furthermost sheets, so he joined in the chase, too.

"The paper chase," she heard him quip and gritted her teeth at his pun of the celebrated television series.

As they gathered some of the elusive papers Victoria glanced upward to see her students clustering around the second story windows of the main-house. They peered down on the three of them with laughing fascination, waving and gesturing.

A window was swept open and Doris Everman leaned out. "Do you need me to come and help?" she called gaily.

The meaningful manner in which Victoria straightened and lifted her head hushed the tittering. It also left Doris in no doubt about what would follow if she didn't return to her work. The window was promptly closed.

The little busybodies! Victoria fumed, her vexation mounting. Giving this disgraceful show for Clifford Pennington was bad enough, but for them, too? Any advantage she had with the attorney, *if* she had ever had one, was certainly shattered to nonexistence now. After this gauche display he would never take her seriously!

If Clifford would have admitted it, especially after his disagreeable telephone conversation with Victoria Carroll the day before, he had come to Brayntree possessing his own expectations of what the other half-owner looked like. He had pictured her a robust, large-bosomed woman with squared fingernails, practical shoes and a plain functional wristwatch. Her walk, he imagined, would be heavy and determined, threatening to all men.

Watching Victoria now as she bent for a scrap of pink paper, he guessed her breasts would be high and full and as delicately pale as her throat. He found himself pausing to admire the fine shape of her knees. As she inadvertently twisted from her waist, even beneath the jacket he glimpsed perfectly shaped hips and slender legs. She bent again, and the hem of her dress slipped innocently to mid-thigh.

Though he didn't actually fancy himself as a

veteran girl watcher, he went achingly taut at the unexpected allure of her. As another paper skittered past him he moved forward to grasp it, unable to concentrate on anything except the curves of Victoria's conveniently displayed behind.

At the precise moment that he stooped, Victoria also saw the movement of the same paper. She turned, reaching for it, too.

It was one of those moments when they saw the inevitable touching but couldn't stop the body motion nearly soon enough. Her shoulder gouged Clifford in the long hard muscle running down the side of his leg. To prevent himself from falling he thrust one hand outward. Since he was half crouched, he stumbled slightly forward. As Victoria groped upward at the same time, the sharp bone framing his eyebrow clipped her painfully in the center of her lower lip.

"Oooh!" she cried and unconsciously clawed her fingernails into his suitcoat.

All thoughts of the papers were instantly forgotten as she slumped to kneel onto the carpet of leaves. She closed one hand over her hurting mouth. For several moments she rocked back and forth in keenest agony.

"Here," he insisted anxiously and dropped to one knee. "Let me see."

Both of them were heedless of the fact that he virtually straddled her knees as he took her by the shoulders and balanced his weight on his heels. He muttered gutteral, sympathetic sounds meant to be an apology but which seemed to only worsen her anguish.

Presently, as the pain subsided a bit, Victoria became aware of Clifford's glaring intimacy. He was touching her temple, urging her to let him inspect what damage had been done, brushing back the disheveled locks tumbling across her eyes. At the same time he endeavored to pry her hand from her mouth.

It was the drugging male smell of him that jolted her to her senses. She was sitting motionless, growing irrationally, unforgivably, drunk with the scent of a man who would close her school and leave her homeless. She was mad!

Viciously she slapped at his hand. "I'm all right!" she yelped out her muffled protest. "Leave me alone."

"Oh, be still," he ordered hoarsely.

Now she truly refused to cooperate. Horrified, she glanced to the vicinity of her knees at the masterful spread of his legs and the distinctly muscled thighs, the neat outline of the crotch of his trousers. *This wasn't happening!*

Clifford trapped both her jaws in the palm of one hand.

"Blast you, Pennington, that hurts!" she lashed out as he shoved her flailing hand away. "I see the secret of your success. Assault and battery."

Scowling down at her, he twisted his mouth into a disapproving grimace. "Women who call men by their surnames deserve to be hit. If I hadn't already done so, I would probably do it now," he threatened drily.

As the realtor methodically plodded about the lawn, thanklessly retrieving the contents of the file, Clifford pinned Victoria's most dangerous arm to her side. As he bent over her mouth his open jacket brushed her bared knees. She wasn't certain which subdued her more: the throb in her lip, or the nonchalant possessiveness of this strange man.

"A nasty little cut," he observed. "Your teeth must be as sharp as your tongue."

"Agh!" she gagged as he plucked out the edge of her lip in a most unflattering scrutiny of the cut.

She moaned another incoherent complaint which he totally ignored. Touching the corner of his clean handkerchief to the tiny wound, he blotted the blood once, then again.

He wasn't just touching her. He was invading her. Holding her jaws as he was, the gasps of her breathing thrust her breasts firmly against his forearm. He had to be aware of it, yet he didn't appear the least inclined to release her.

In a feeble effort to salvage some of her poise, Victoria closed the fingers of one hand firmly about his wrist. It was larger, harder, much more powerful than hers. The dominating male potential beneath the brittle cuff was reassuring, yet terrifying in its unfamiliarity. This man was a stranger, she thought with wonder; an unknown person stroking her with the ease of a friend of many years. It wasn't right. It wasn't proper. It was most certainly dangerous.

As if she voiced some lament, some panic which alerted him, Clifford paused. He quickly drew back as he released her jaw. Over the inches which separated them, their confused impressions confronted each other. Her eyes, clear and artless, said, *But I don't know you.* His, golden and puzzled, replied, *I want to understand what has happened here.*

Clifford leaned back on his heels, and she clearly recognized his superior strength, his longer years of experience. Yet his breath, when she surrendered for that one moment, came roughly, as if she were the victor.

"You should put ice on that," he advised solemnly, "or you'll have a tender mouth in the morning."

She lowered her eyes from his perplexed scrutiny but flicked them back again, shuttered, aloof, once again in control. "My mouth isn't really one of your concerns."

His slow grin appeared almost relieved that she had broken the bewitching current. He was boyish and not at all the attorney with his white teeth gleaming beneath the moustache, so interestingly uneven on the bottom. "Why, that's a real pity, Victoria," he chuckled.

The past moments were unlike any Victoria had ever experienced. The frightened girl in her sharpened her words. "Spare me the levities, Pennington," she retorted and averted her face. Tenderly she probed at her lip.

Arising in one graceful motion, she inspected the extent of her injury with the tip of her small pink tongue. In her preoccupation with this unwittingly sensual ritual she failed to see the muscle flexing repeatedly in Clifford's jaw. He, too, rose, his gaze fastened on her. Nor did she observe the attorney's disturbed shift of weight as he scowled and jammed one hand deep into his pocket.

As Victoria halfheartedly smiled at the rumpled realtor returning with the jumble of her file, Clifford sighed and squinted into the glare of the sun. He stared at some vague point far past the hulking edifice of Brayntree. Suddenly he was displeased with himself.

Twenty-four hours ago the litigation had been clear-cut and simple. Now it was unexpectedly complicated. He wasn't certain whether his disquiet was because he felt a puzzling compassion for the straits of this woman's circumstances or not. He suspected it was because she was the most confoundingly desirable woman he had ever seen in his life, including a number of lovely women whose names he could hardly remember. And—he found the thought troubling—his fiancée of two years.

Faith Chambers would be dumbfounded if she had any inkling of how hotly aroused he had grown at the mere sight of Victoria Carroll's legs. For one thing, Faith wouldn't believe it, since the passion which existed between them was . . . merely comfortable —a deep friendship, a genuine respect, little more.

Victoria Carroll was one thing he would never attempt to explain to Faith. He wasn't certain if he could even explain her to himself.

The next hour and a half was a disoriented block of time out of Victoria's life which was lost to her forever. She reacted purely by instinct. Her body moved with an involuntary process which was separated entirely from her conscious thoughts. Like someone at a funeral who obediently walks where she is told to, sits when she is pushed down onto a chair, Victoria only breathed and remained alive.

As the two men wandered somewhere about the estate doing whatever it was that attorneys and realtors did, the morning's classes were dismissed. The girls clumped boisterously down the stairs, chattered about clothes and boys through the central corridor and happily proceeded to lunch. Doris Everman ran true to form on her trek across the main floor. She ducked her curly head into Victoria's office and shot her an exaggerated, slapstick wink.

"He's a livin' doll, Miss Carroll. No false teeth and no bald head. Lock him in the attic, and I'll take him his meals. Oh, what a hunk!"

Victoria had been leaning against one of the

ceiling-to-floor bookcases visualizing abhorrent streams of buyers parading through Brayntree's rooms. They left dirty footprints and slammed doors. They lifted panels of the draperies and rubbed them between their fingers, sniffed in disdain and moved on to criticize something else.

"What?" she asked, distracted.

"I said Mr. Pennington has raised everyone's blood pressure. Is something the matter, ma'am?"

Victoria smiled unhappily. "Oh no, Doris. Everything's fine. Really. I'm just a little tired, that's all."

Doris sobered, and her sidelong look seemed insulted, as if she didn't believe a word of it. "I'll have Mamie fix you a tray and bring it to you myself, Miss Carroll."

"Hmm? Oh, yes. That would be nice, Doris. Thank you."

With a grimace that supremely suited the wild rebellion of her hair, Doris withdrew.

She was Brayntree's Mistress, Victoria mused. She was The Brave Teacher. Moving to the tall windows to gaze out at Clifford's Porsche parked arrogantly in the drive, somewhere deep inside her, a part of the teacher drifted, became lost. It had nothing whatsoever to do with Brayntree.

"What a fool you are, Victoria," she accused herself.

Up until this morning she had privately scoffed at the term "chemistry" between a man and a woman. Liking was liking and loving was loving. A woman liked many people and loved her family and her husband. Somehow, in her ignorance, she had equated loving a man with the same goodness with which she had loved her mother. Different, yes, but not *that* different.

She experienced a brief flash of herself kneeling

with Clifford's sinewy legs straddling her knees. He held her face in his hand, and the tableau solidified, framed into a permanent part of her memory. She trembled uncontrollably.

Chemistry? The knifelike awareness which had slashed through her mind at his touch had carved a mysterious hold inside her. It was the craving for a smell she could never recapture. It was a hunger to touch the vigor of muscles and flesh that she could not satisfy with her imagination. It was an addict's blissful high that could never be achieved except by taking another dose and another and another until she could no longer live without it.

Then you're hooked, she thought. *Hooked on a man. In love.*

When the door whispered open behind her she said, "Just put the tray on the desk, Doris. Thank you."

She knew, the second the words were uttered, that he was in the room. She felt his presence like the pressure of a storm in the air. Everything was changed: the room, the space, the light, the sound of the blaze crackling in the fireplace and the rushing warmth of her own body.

Spinning about, she threw up a guard over her face and tried to pretend the difference did not exist.

They stood on opposite sides of the room. Neither of them moved. Only the look spun out like a thread—a steel cable—to hang between them. Victoria made her eyes say she didn't care, that she could look at him and not care or desire more. Then she felt foolish and forced a smile.

"Have you finished what you came to do?"

"I'm not sure that is possible," he replied, then tightened his mouth until fine grooves cut down the sides of his face. He disregarded his own allusion to the magnetism. "Please know that I would like to see your interests protected in all of this."

As he drew the tip of an index finger across the line of his moustache he let his eyes roam over her face. But he carefully prevented them from straying any lower.

"Really?" She snapped the words without thinking. Closing her eyes, she pinched the bridge of her nose. She lifted her head without opening her eyes and said dully, "My mother taught me many things. One was to depend only on myself when the going gets rough." Her eyes flew open. "I consider this rough."

Clifford flicked the button to his suitcoat and it fell open. The vest fit him magnificently, tapering to his slender waist and barely touching his trousers as they hugged his hips. He glanced about the large room as if he were immensely uncomfortable. She did nothing to relieve it, offered him nothing, not even to take a seat.

"Ed will be finished in a few minutes," he assured her. "I'll send you the results as soon as he gives them to me. Ed Barnes is good. He'll give us a fair estimate."

She laughed bitterly. "What I'm worth, you mean? What this place is worth? What my mother's grave is worth?"

He didn't reply to such pain. He couldn't reply.

Victoria stepped to her desk and automatically arranged things which were already in perfect order. "The plumbing is a disaster, you know. Every winter something bursts and we have a flood in the basement. The oven can be counted on to burn out once a year. And the staff? Two women, three men and an extra teacher?"

Her look ripped him to ruthless shreds. "Please

tell Mr. Barnes to temper his figures with the human element. I'm in debt up to my earlobes, Pennington. The utilities on this place alone—"

"Victoria—"

She took a panicky step backward, fearing his sympathy more than his commitment to his duty.

"Send your papers," she said thickly. "Make your phone calls to Eliot. I'll handle my own affairs in my own way." When she shook her head her hair glittered and flounced about her cheeks. Her bones were finely sculpted beneath the sensitive skin, and they lifted with injustice. "But I won't stand for it very nicely, Pennington. You can't expect me to do that."

Clifford looked very tired. His long, tanned fingers fished in an inside pocket and withdrew a business card. With no apologies in his gait, he stepped toward her. His gaze was veiled. She couldn't possibly guess what he thought. With a grip that was almost painful, he grasped her hand from her side and slapped the card into its palm. Then he bent the delicate fingers closed. But he didn't release her hand.

"If you get into trouble with the banks . . ."

She started to interrupt, but he inclined his head to silence her. "If you get into trouble, give me a call. I have some contacts who might consider Brayntree a good investment. Anyway, let me know if there's anything I can do."

Before the tears could well in her eyes she withdrew her hand and turned toward the window. How much, much simpler all this would have been if he had only been the realtor.

Clifford shifted his weight to one foot, slouching gracefully, memorizing her back, the elegant taper of her calves in their smart leather boots. His eyes darted to the window, back to her, to the desk, then fell upon a tiny snapshot of her tucked beneath the edge of a paperholder. It was a delightful, laughing picture of her sitting Indian fashion on the sandy beach of the peninsula.

He hesitated, then glanced at her rigid posture one more time. Moistening his lips, he quickly slipped the picture into his pocket.

The door closed with a faint click which cut them apart with the neat precision of a well-stropped razor. If she were lucky, she would never see him again except at the hearing for Eliot's petition. If she were lucky she would only suffer a few sleepless nights.

She didn't want to watch him leave so she walked in a meticulously careful line toward the door. She would go to her room. Then no one would see her when she cried.

Chapter Three

Two hundred thousand dollars!

Neat rows of typescript quivered across the page of letterhead stationery which trembled in Victoria's hand. Pennington and Associates, the stately print declared at the top. Dear Miss Carroll . . .

Alone in her office for the first time in hours, Victoria furiously skimmed the letter again. Eliot Carroll was entitled to nearly a quarter of a million dollars from Brayntree's solvent assets, it ruthlessly informed her. Some faceless stenographer named "c.l." had transcribed her death warrant from a page of dictation which was probably crumpled in a wastebasket by now. Across the bottom Clifford's signature swept in a bold, arrogant scrawl. With the tip of one polished fingernail she traced the aggressive path of his pen.

For the past week the memory of his touch had

haunted her more than she liked to admit. Her days had persisted in winding up vaguely off center, without purpose. She had even deteriorated to the point of daydreaming about him. She, in her discreet virgin's way, had been behaving like one of her idol-struck students ooh-ing and aah-ing over Robert Redford.

And now this! Ed Barnes should have his realtor's license revoked for such a flagrantly unfair assessment, and Clifford Pennington should be disbarred for supporting such a claim. If she were less a judge of human nature she would figure they were in it together, pulling off one of those notorious land swindling scams. But she knew better than that. The figures, she supposed, were uncontestable. She couldn't help but believe, however, that if she weren't a "defenseless woman" the assessment would have inclined a little more in her favor.

All of this left her exactly three choices, none of them promising. Retain Brian Levy and fight it in court, locate Eliot and try to reason with him, or try to attain a loan from some source and buy Eliot out completely.

At this moment she despised every precious ounce of energy she had squandered fantasizing about Clifford Pennington, lying awake wondering what it would be like to be kissed by him, to be held in his arms for real, of how his legs would feel naked and smoothly entwined with hers. Now, after the letter, she felt like a traitor to Brayntree. She was ashamed and bitterly disgusted with herself.

Half crushing the letter, Victoria stood before the window and stared at the consoling majesty of the trees. Except for the pendant which she monotonously slipped back and forth on its chain, she didn't move when Stephanie walked into the room.

"Reading that letter a hundred times won't solve anything, you know," the assistant teacher uselessly advised her.

"I can't help it. I just can't accept that this is happening to us. There must be a way to stop it, something I'm overlooking."

"It's happening, and you're doing all anyone can do. Are you going to teach the girls how to alter a dress pattern today, or shall I send them over to the gym for their aerobics?"

Victoria turned, her slim shoulders drooping. "Aerobics, I suppose. But should I send them home is the real question. Or perhaps I should just hang myself from the tallest tree and end the torture quickly."

Giving her superior a swift inspection, Stephanie saw everything at a glance: the tweed slacks and beige cableknit sweater which fit more loosely than usual, the paleness which made Victoria's delicate complexion appear almost translucent, the smudged shadows beneath weary eyes, the sensual, stubborn mouth.

She removed the letter from Victoria's hand and tossed it aside. Stephanie was accustomed to fighting crises; she never wasted energy fighting the impossible.

"Well," she said with a brisk sigh, "what's your next move?"

"To make the rounds to the banks, I suppose. I'll call upon our illustrious Mr. Stampley and cross my legs and endure the routine about how no trouble would dare happen to Brayntree if Mother were alive. One thing I'm doing is informing Mr. Pennington what he can do with his joke of an assessment."

Moving to the wall of bookshelves, Stephanie

pulled out a volume of Plato. She rummaged behind it to produce a pack of extra slim cigarettes. Elegantly lighting one, she blew a slender column of smoke toward the ceiling, her one secret escape valve.

"Let Brian Levy handle everything," she advised. "I know you'd like to take the realtor to task, but he's only an innocent party."

"Brian is getting so senile it's a wonder to me how he manages to get dressed every morning."

Stephanie shrugged. "Retain someone else."

"For Mother's sake I hate to."

After an uneventful pause Stephanie spoke quietly. "I know Clifford Pennington."

Victoria was half-heartedly attempting to revive the fire. Startled at the remark, she pivoted, the poker thrust out from her hand like a poised rapier prepared for battle.

"Why didn't you tell me before?" she breathed.

Stephanie concentrated on her cigarette. "I didn't realize it until I got a good look at him, Victoria. His name meant nothing to me. I used to know a woman who . . . who was once involved with him. Oh, it was a long time ago."

As Victoria's thoughts splintered into a jumbled collage of bewilderment, an obscure sense of betrayal and annoyance, she noisily replaced the poker. "This woman," she began overcasually as her anger took on a new aspect, "she was a close friend?"

"Uh-hm."

Victoria urged her again, pretending an assured, blasé laugh this time. "Well, that's not fair. What did they do, for pity's sake? Have an affair? Of course, that would be expected—a man like him."

Stephanie crushed out her cigarette and adjusted her dress, indicating she really must return to the students. "I don't think anyone really knew exactly what they did. My friend thought they would marry, or so she told me. I got the feeling she would have had to stand in line. Why?"

The younger woman smiled with a shrug. "No reason."

The sound Stephanie made between her teeth was pointedly disbelieving. "Then why press?"

"I wasn't pressing! I merely asked a simple question! Mr. Pennington is one of those spoiled, educated men who has everything given to him from the day he is born. He can have a dozen affairs. It doesn't matter to me one way or another."

Pausing with one hand on the doorfacing, the other woman stood mutely until Victoria lifted her face. When Stephanie grinned an amused smirk, Victoria pursed her mouth with unconscious prettiness.

"If you say so," Stephanie intoned. "But I doubt there's anything simple about it. 'Methinks thou dost protest too much,' Victoria."

Victoria aimed what she hoped was a humorously critical finger at her secretary. "You have far too many magazines stuffed under your mattress, Steph. Stop concocting fairytales or I'll tell your mother."

The other woman was still laughing when she pulled the door shut behind her.

Victoria watched, but didn't see, the door closing. For several moments she stood motionless. As she thoughtfully lowered her hand to her side it clinched into a small tight fist. Her eyes glistened, richly brown, dark like newly-turned earth caught in the shadows. No trace of a smile lingered on her face.

Brian Levy's office reflected his middle-aged personality the way a woman's kitchen translates the barometer of her moods. At least a year had passed

since Victoria had last come here, then to sadly
attend to Helen's affairs.

The same dozens of photographs proudly decorated the wall behind Levy—a splendidly prolific display of grinning, snaggle-toothed grandchildren with
toddling great-grandchildren in various states of
dress and undress. In the background were their
more sedate parents standing or sitting beside their
spouses.

"You will live forever, Mr. Levy," Victoria attempted meaningless pleasantries two weeks later as
she removed her leather coat and draped it over a
chair in the old man's office.

The lawyer chuckled. "There will always be a
Levy in Virginia, I agree."

Victoria took a seat beside the window which
looked out from six floors up. Winter had come
early, as she had forecast. Williamsburg's sky was as
gray as steel. It drooped heavily with a mist so fine
that the restored buildings and landmarks in the
distance became lost in foggy obscurity.

When the capital had moved to Richmond in 1780
the town had slumped into a decline. It took the
John D. Rockefeller fortune to restore the historical
sites and preserve the heritage. People like Brian
Levy were part of that heritage, living half their lives
in the past. So she played out the small ceremony of
removing her gloves and smoothing them flat upon
her shoulder bag. She sat very straight, since Mr.
Levy was of the opinion that southern women
shouldn't slouch, roast themselves brown under the
sun, wear pants in public or use slang.

Victoria's three-piece wool suit was deliberately
feminine. Her fingernails were manicured perfectly,
her makeup clear and natural. Today she was a
genteel southern pillar of tradition. As the silver-

haired man smoked a cigar—a blessedly mild one—
she took a full ten minutes to pour out her story of
Brayntree's misfortune.

"There must be something I can do," she finished
with a prudent balance between a helpless belle and
a liberated business woman. "I've been to every
banker in town. They all looked at me as if I were
insane. No one wants to lend a single woman
$200,000 when she has only one source of income."

Mr. Levy shook his head as if he agreed with the
bankers.

"Eliot promised me we could work this out together. I want you to file a counter petition or
something. Breach of promise."

"I don't think Eliot is being malicious. He probably is desperate for money. Times are hard."

"Well, what about me? I'm more than desperate."

"What does Pennington say?"

Victoria sniffed haughtily. "Pennington? In my
opinion that man is unethical."

"Clifford Pennington?" the distracted man
mused. He flicked some ashes into a tray on his desk
and leaned far back in his chair. His descriptive
gestures were eloquently sketched with the tip of his
cigar. "Stubborn, maybe, but clean as a whistle. I
know that boy well."

She winced. "He's hardly a boy."

"Born the same year as our David." He indicated
a specific photograph behind him. "Fine boy, Clifford. Graduated summa cum laude, you know.
From what I hear, William and Mary College is
proud to have him on the staff, even on a limited
basis. He's writing a book, I hear. Of course," he
sighed as if he didn't entirely agree with the newer
trends, "all Ph.D.'s have to be published nowa-
days."

Not expecting this at all, yet not really surprised, Victoria rose abruptly to pace the floor. Brian didn't appear to notice how pinched her mouth was or how tenaciously her fingers were laced and twisted. When she caught her breath to interrupt his unwittingly cruel reminiscing, he charged on.

"Cliff's mother was a Philmore. Daughter of old Stephen Philmore. When Madeline married Ethan Pennington—we went to that wedding, Betty and I. Splendid affair. They had an out-of-town florist, though. We did think that was carrying things a bit too far. Williamsburg had a perfectly fine florist over on Vine Street. Anyway, let's see . . . where was I? Oh, yes. Ethan started the law firm with his younger brother. Half the houses in Williamsburg didn't even have electricity then. Ah, those were the days. I often think—"

"Mr. Levy—"

"Yep," Brian said and slapped his thigh. He innocently adjusted his chair and tucked his spectacles upon his nose. He took up some scribbled notes he had made as Victoria had related her tale. Just as Victoria thought he was about to give her some professional advice at last, he removed the glasses and leaned back in his chair again.

"Cliff's made himself a fine match. No doubt about that. Chambers, I think the girl's name is. Don't know much about her mother's people, but her grandfather was a city commissioner for years. Son of Joshua Chambers—tobacco farmers, all of 'em. The family goes back to the first settlers, if I'm not sadly mistaken." He smiled at her apologetically. "Of course, I'd have to look that up. My memory's not what it used to be."

Whirling from before the window, Victoria flashed him a dazzling smile. She reached for her coat without explaining that she couldn't listen to any more, without telling him that she couldn't feel the slightest sympathy for Clifford or she was lost. She awkwardly tugged on the coat. Distracted, she fumbled to button it, but her hands shook so badly she grabbed up her bag.

At the sight of her preparing to leave, Brian's face fell as if he didn't understand and, of course, he couldn't. He watched her yank on her gloves, frowning.

"You must forgive me," she muttered and didn't hesitate to tell the lie, not for herself but for Helen. "I'm late for another appointment which I entirely miscalculated."

Her strides toward the door were rapid and uneven.

"Don't you even want me to draft a letter to Eliot and see if we can't work out some settlement out of court?" he called after her, rising from his seat. "I'd have to go through young Pennington, naturally, but it's the logical first step. These things take time. I don't want you to worry about it. I'll take care of everything."

This man had been Helen's dear friend and an invaluable advisor for years. He really cared about what happened to Victoria, and she knew it. To tell him that he was incapable of helping her, that he would actually hurt her, was unthinkable. She swallowed down her despair.

"I may have an alternative," she explained in a dull monotone. "A private loan, perhaps. I don't know. I'll get back to you. But don't . . . do anything yet."

"Whatever you say, of course," he agreed. He gave her the courtly respect of accompanying her to the door. "But it does seem to me as if Cliff gave you some sound advice. Think of what you could do with your half of the estate in cash, Victoria. Why, you could buy one of those nice convenient apartments all the young ladies are raving about."

Wrenching open the door, protest shrieking in her head like a maelstrom, she strode swiftly toward the elevator. But at the last moment she feared she would only arouse the inquisitive gawking of anyone who saw her. She continued walking, almost running to the stairway.

She just *couldn't* end up crawling to Clifford for help! It wasn't only that he had whetted some unacceptable hunger within her; infatuation—if that was what it had been—had a miraculous way of dying if it was starved long enough. But she and Helen had remained independent for too many years. She wasn't accustomed to asking for favors and waiting for some man behind a desk to finally pick up a phone or write a letter. If something needed doing, one of them did it.

The stairs weren't far away, and she clattered down six exhausting flights. As her small feet skittered down the steps the warning logic sounded over and over in her head, like a ruined phonograph needle skating repetitiously on its track. *You have no choice. You have no choice. You have no choice.*

Agitated almost beyond reason, she took the Colonial Parkway west, driving directly toward Brayntree. Moist ringlets still fell about her face from her headlong dash down the stairs. For once the drafty interior of her jeep was comforting.

A thin film of mist beaded on the windshield, occasionally forming a rivulet to drizzle down the glass. The tires hissed familiarly on the pavement and only intensified the battle waging in her mind. Her whole world seemed tilted on its axis. Only two weeks ago everything had moved along in its steady routine fashion: Doris misbehaved, Victoria juggled bills, and Stephanie only backslid to her nicotine habit once in a while. Now? She was forced to appeal to the opposition.

"I don't trust you, Pennington," she declared aloud to the accompaniment of the windshield wipers. "I'd almost rather lose."

She drove a good twenty minutes before she whipped the jeep off the highway and onto the graded shoulder. The tires skidded to a stop with short spurts of crunching gravel. The engine, after whining to a halt, rumbled with its customary grumpiness.

Victoria's forehead dropped forward to rest upon the knuckles of her fingers circling the steering wheel. "Oh, Lord, I have to do it, don't I? There is no other way. Oh, my. Oh my, oh my."

She dreaded approaching Clifford so badly her stomach knotted with dull, aching rebellion. Automatically glancing behind her—fortunately the highway was deserted since she wasn't paying the slightest attention to what she was doing—she made a U-turn. She pulled up to the first public telephone booth she found.

With the card Clifford had given her lying in a folded and mutilated condition on the shelf, she dropped in her quarter. It clinked with thoughtless cheerfulness to the bottom of the phone. After punching out the digits with gloved fingers, she waited and began to tremble.

A woman's voice answered. "I'm sorry, but Mr. Pennington is out of the office for the remainder of the afternoon. This is his day at the college. May I help you?"

"Oh?" Victoria replied at a loss. She pressed her

lips with her fingertips, wishing she could take this as some omen and call the whole thing off. "It's all right," she said. "I'll catch him another time."

But another time would not do. There was no more time.

Finding Clifford was much too easy. Room 23 in an annex to the left of the Administration Building of William and Mary College was conveniently accessible. Victoria stood at one end of an empty corridor and stared at the glass rectangle in Clifford's classroom door. It beckoned to her over the distance. It challenged her like the disastrous lid to Pandora's box.

She inched nearer, then a bit nearer still. Inside that room, she thought, was the man who had helped make her life a sudden shambles. Inside was the one man in the whole wretched world who had dared to melt her with a look, the man who would gaze at her now with condescending triumph and say, *You've done the right thing in coming to me for help.*

Standing on tiptoe, she forced herself to peep inside.

Clifford was leaning back against the front edge of his desk, his hips braced securely, his long legs clad in sharply creased denim jeans and crossed at the ankles. His turtle-necked sweater was folded down beneath a gently obstinate jaw, and his tweed sport jacket was casually unbuttoned.

A wrinkled paper was clasped in the same hand which balanced itself on the surface of the desk. He was the picture of leisured elegance, a man who was happily enjoying the charm of his sexuality. He smiled at his class with the luxury of one whose contentment could afford to be generous.

More than a dozen entranced feminine faces

gazed up at him; their legs were crossed, their books were open, a few pens were working. The young men listened with respectful attentiveness. The sight of Clifford's profile seemed to solidify the air around her. She stiffened. It wasn't right! It was hatefully unfair! What had she done to deserve everything she had ever wanted thrown into jeopardy while he lived his life so damned easily?

Harsh fingers of hysteria clawed at her throat, and she knew she couldn't go through with the charade, not with him. She didn't care what she had to call it. Pride? Yes, she admitted it; she was selfishly, unreasonably, inflexibly proud! She would not beg him, not even for Brayntree!

Unfortunately, one of the female students in the first row glimpsed Victoria's slight movement. Her flicker of distraction drew the attention of the professor as he made his point. In less time than it took for Victoria to decide she had made a mistake in coming, he caught the twist of her copper-gilded head.

If Victoria hadn't been conscious of drawing notice of herself she would have dashed out of the building in a flurry. But, as luck would have it, a young man about her own age strolled nonchalantly from the opposite end of the hall. When he approached he smiled courteously and she couldn't run then. Her heels clattered clearly on the tiles as she hurried. When her name echoed down the hallway she flinched, but didn't turn around.

"Victoria!"

The young man looked her squarely in the eye. One of his sandy brows lifted inquisitively. He gestured to a long-legged figure which Victoria knew was close behind her. "If you're Victoria," he grinned, "you're being paged. Good afternoon, Dr. Pennington."

"Hello, Jeff," Clifford's deep voice resonated from just behind Victoria's shoulder. "Damn it, Victoria," he muttered in a hushed command. "Will you slow down for a flaming minute?"

Escape was out of the question.

Clifford's fingers, when they bit leanly into the flesh of her shoulder, were different than when he had touched her before. Then he had been anxious; now he was possessive and demanding. She recognized her awkward disadvantage. She was on *his* home turf and she had peered through *his* door. Extracting herself from this situation with dignity was unlikely.

He towered over her, irritable and puzzled. "You heard me call you," he accused. "Why didn't you stop?"

The muscles in her neck tightened viciously. She thrashed in her mind for a reasonably believable answer. Before she could think of an excuse he added, "And you can cut all the garbage you're getting ready to dump on me, Victoria. The truth will do nicely."

"I'm not *here*, Pennington," she answered him with a pretended calm. "I'm on my way *from* here. There's a difference. Something came up. I had to change my mind."

For a moment his narrow-eyed inspection continued to scour over her discomfort. Her chin tipped upward and brought the finely locked bones of her face into prominence. He could have traced them with a fingertip.

The vibrations which had cross-circuited between them before at Brayntree had not diminished; if anything they were more dangerous. Victoria held herself aloofly correct, hoping as she did so that her manner would distract him. When his look slid to her rigid shoulders and hands she realized he had cleverly read through her pretenses.

"Semantics is my strong suit, sweetheart," he said in a light joking manner. He released her arm. "I daresay you could never best me."

Victoria went limp with relief that he was not pinning her down. She coughed. "I wouldn't try. But fighting hopeless odds is my strong suit. You know the old saying about fools rushing in." She was chattering, but it was better than enduring the silence in the deserted hallway. "That's me—a fool. Nice, but a fool." She smiled, then suddenly sobered.

When she finally ceased jabbering he lifted one appraising eyebrow. His tongue moved thoughtfully across his upper lip to graze the edge of his moustache.

"That was some speech," he admitted, grinning boyishly.

She lowered her eyes.

"You're anything but a fool, Miss Carroll," he went on, "so don't try to play me for one."

"You make me nervous."

"Why?"

"Don't cross-examine me, Pennington!" she snapped. "I'm not on trial. Look, I have to go."

He buttoned his jacket with unconscious finality. "Nonsense. You're here now. I'll dismiss my class, then we can go somewhere and talk."

She must have looked as if she would cry, because he softened his abrasive manner. The aggressive angle of his chin relented a bit. The sinewed strength in his shoulders slowly relaxed. With a low whistling sound, he let out his breath, considering her, crinkling the lines about his eyes. Again she noticed the fascinating unevenness of his lower teeth.

Not wanting to give in, she wet her lips. The smile she yielded was considerably more congenial than her flashes of temper.

Clifford saw she was weakening. "See?" he teased. "You're not the only one who fights hopeless odds."

Thinking it was settled, Clifford took several steps in the direction of his classroom. Victoria, now that he couldn't see her, indulged in the liberty of watching the sensual, loose-jointed way he moved, the smooth runner's swing of his arms that played tricks with her senses. She really did want to talk to him, and not just because of Brayntree. But she couldn't run the risk of losing control before a roomful of college students. As rattled as she was at this moment, she would ruin herself.

Half turning, she began inching backward toward the exit at the opposite end of the hall.

"Don't-do-that-Victoria," he ordered wearily without looking at her.

She wanted to hate him for reading her so easily! She hurled a gaze burning with resentment at the superior reflection in his eyes.

As he waited for her grudging steps to fall in with his, he said, "You didn't get the money, did you?"

The words couldn't have been more ill-timed. They rained on her like pelting blows, damaging her now-fragile pride. Her jaw clamped in wounded affront. She stopped short.

Her censure blamed him more because it was so trembling and quiet, aimed at the center of his chest. "Oh, Pennington," she said sorrowfully, the words tearing, "you should have let me say it. You should have at least left me that much."

He didn't reply. She heard his slow, deep breaths and had no idea of what he thought.

She jerked up her head. "I can't stay here," she declared recklessly. "Later. I may call later. Maybe never."

Clifford stepped in front of her so quickly that she couldn't avoid touching him. His shoulder jostled hers, and she went achingly, instantly limp. The emptiness of the hallway alarmed her terribly; she could feel the warmth of his breath brushing her cheeks. He didn't touch her with his hands, though he might as well have when his nearness drained the strength from her legs. She was terrified someone would see them.

"My name is Clifford," he ground tightly. "Will you, for once, not dig your grave with your teeth, Victoria? Why are you so proud to admit you need me? I can help you. Where the hell is the difficulty in that?"

"I don't want your help."

"Wanting and needing are two different things," he said uselessly.

Knowing that neither of them were admitting the real reason of the conflict, he sighed and dropped his arms to his sides. He glanced dejectedly at the wall, then back. Placing a bent knuckle against the curve of her jaw, he rotated her face until it was even with his.

"I feel it, too," he said with astonishing honesty. "And I didn't ask to feel it any more than you did."

A vision of another woman locked in his arms blazed through Victoria's mind; its image hurt her physically, like a fist in the stomach.

Before she thought she lifted her fingers and pressed their tips upon his lips. "Don't say it," she whispered.

The warm firmness of his mouth, the crisp bristle of his moustache, the instantaneous stiffening of his body shocked her more than any blow of a fist.

She snatched back her hand. "I'm sorry!" she choked, her eyes flared and amazed.

His lashes fluttered downward. Their thick frill outlined the cleanly-hewn blades of his cheekbones. Something—she could have sworn it was physical— passed through him. A shudder, a resignation, a yielding up of something he wanted: she didn't know. She knew she must say something, anything.

"You should get back to class," she advised quickly and with forced brightness. "Your students have paid a lot of money to see your . . . genius at work."

It was just the right rudeness to rescue them. As he opened his guarded eyes to see her girlish, coaxing smile, the edges of his own mouth twitched in amusement. He moved to the door and inclined his head in a royal invitation.

"Let me amaze you with my expertise then," he said, which meant, *Thank you for doing that.*

Victoria had no choice except to meet his strained pleasantry with that of her own. "A person just doesn't tell you no, do they?"

He extended an arm over her head to brace open the door. As she slipped warily beneath the powerful canopy of his sleeve, she barely heard his murmured retort.

"You're the first in a long time, my pet," he chuckled.

Chapter Four

*W*hen Victoria stood within the curious environment of Clifford's classroom, the unwilling object of all those puzzled pairs of eyes, she suffered her first true guilt over Faith Chambers. *I am pretending,* she thought. *I'm a fraud standing here in front of all these people, behaving as if he means no more to me than any other man.*

She had never demeaned herself by being a fraud before. Helen Carroll had schooled her rigorously in matters of propriety. A gentlewoman meticulously avoided situations which could be misconstrued. A woman who made her living off the respect and trust of the public ran from the faintest breath of scandal. A woman was correct, for her own sake.

Now, in this particular situation, complicated by the fact that she was as pretty as any woman in the room (she didn't bury her head in the sand about the disadvantage of that factor) she felt the danger. The

gorgeous professor sprinting down the hall to bring
back a pretty young woman? Who would believe the
innocence of that?

"Is this your fiancée, Dr. Pennington?" inquired a
thin-voiced boy almost at the same instant of someone's vigorously loud *shush*.

If the typical college-kid question threw Clifford
off balance, his acting was unsurpassed. An embarrassed crimson immediately betrayed Victoria's pretended calm. The look she telegraphed the unruffled
professor beside the desk was one of pure horror.

But Clifford's chin lifted confidently, and the
artful shift of his weight warned Victoria to let him
smooth over the social blunder of his student. As if
giving the question serious consideration, he smiled.
Then he snapped the clasps shut on his case with the
timed delivery of a punch line.

"Unfortunately no, John," he said. "Miss Carroll
is a . . . client. Why, would you like to marry her
yourself?"

John blushed as furiously as Victoria, but the
merriment which tittered through the room diffused
the tension with miraculous ease.

"Well, if he doesn't, I would," piped another male
voice from the safe anonymity of the rear of the
room.

Again, they laughed.

Clifford unobtrusively moved nearer Victoria. She
stood in front of his desk, touching its edge for
support. As the relaxing effect of good humor
loosened up the room his fingers brushed against
hers, a featherlight urging to go with the changing
mood, to smile and laugh at herself, to beat them at
their own game.

Victoria's shy smile eroded the suspicion of even

the wary-eyed female students. They sat quite still and grudgingly offered her their attitudes to be programmed and won over, at least on a superficial level out of respect for Clifford Pennington.

Aiming her teasing remark at the back row of grinning young men, Victoria arched her brows with very adult sophistication. Giving a worldly flick at her cuff, she laced her words with subtle overtones.

"I'm not easy, sir," she warned.

Over the expected chuckling and teasing banter which, luckily for some of their proponents, did not distinctly reach the professor's ears, Clifford murmured into Victoria's fluff of hair. "Ah, lady, I'd hoped you were."

His provocative suggestion only served to draw the tip of her rapier around to point at him instead of his students. With a sidelong narrowing of her eyes she smilingly promised him that if he wanted to fence in this public place, she wouldn't be quick to back down this time.

He grinned. Grabbing up his heavier jacket from over the back of the chair beside him and tossing it over his shoulder, Clifford dismissed his class. "Have an extra ten minutes on me," he invited generously. "But don't forget final exams in two weeks. I'll have no mercy."

To the accompaniment of quasi-respectful swearing from the men, starry-eyed idolization from a number of the women, desks scraped over the floor. The eager escapees, always takers of a spare moment to grab a snack or smoke an extra cigarette, scooped up their paraphernalia and darted for the door. Clifford adroitly drew Victoria out of the peril of after-class traffic.

"Nice bunch of kids you have there, counselor,"

she remarked over the noise as he stepped to flip off the light switch.

"I try hard," he drawled. He gestured her toward the door.

"Naturally. To get what you want. The Universal Urge of the Male Animal, one of my great aunts calls it. I agree."

His chuckle came from just behind her head. "And just what is it I want, sweetheart?"

She answered without hesitating. "Everything."

Laughing, he propelled her from the room with an unconscious touch upon the small of her back. "Poor baby, don't scowl so. It'll all work out."

Yes, to your advantage, you devil, she agreed silently and preceded him into the hall.

The temperature had dropped at least another five degrees. Shivering, Victoria cast oblique glances at Clifford's taxing strides as they walked to the parking lot. They dodged students hunched beneath backpacks, riding bicycles with their collars folded up, some lugging musical instruments. Clifford's hair ruffled alluringly about his face as he placed her to his inside against the traffic of the street.

After being mistaken for Faith Chambers, Victoria was wary of even walking beside him in public. Yet she knew it was a habit she could quickly acquire. It all felt right: the sensation of being unquestionably *there,* of her movements fitting to his, of being accepted, of belonging. Then she despised her female frailty. How could she be thinking this way? He was the black knight of the piece, or at least one of them—he and Eliot. He was certainly no more the prince than she was the princess.

"Mr. Pennington," she said quickly before he

could interrupt, "if you'd just give me the names of the investors, I could call them myself. Then, if any of them sounds interested and wants to talk to you, I can let you know. I don't want you to go to any more trouble."

He reprimanded her with a dark, raking scowl. "Wrong. Investors like the personal touch of someone they trust. I should talk to them first. Where's your car?"

They stood in the middle of a large asphalt parking lot. People were pouring forth from the surrounding buildings, crowding the wide space.

"Over there." She pointed to her jeep which huddled inconspicuously among all the other ramshackle student vehicles.

Budget-wise Victoria actually could afford to drive something better than a jeep. This particular car was the first car she had ever driven. Helen had bought it for her when she had been learning to drive. The sentimental value made it dear, enhanced by the fact that it literally refused to wear out. She didn't hesitate to take it anywhere, to eat hamburgers with some of the girls or attend a formal concert. Status symbols had nothing to do with it.

Clifford rubbed at his moustache, a habit Victoria was now beginning to realize was his barometer of uneasiness. "The jeep?"

She bridled. "What do you have against jeeps?"

"Everything." He turned up the collar of his jacket and caught her hand. "Come on."

The man's self-confidence was invincible! Smarting from his rejection of her treasured jeep, she trembled as he threaded his fingers through hers and drew her more closely beside him—like friends, which they were not. Yet, she oddly didn't remove her hand. His palm was warm and dry, and as she fell into step she grew acutely conscious of the moist nervousness of her own.

His jeans are too tight, she thought in dismay. *He flaunts his virility the way some men wear a macho chain. He knows exactly how sexy he is.*

She missed her step and bumped against his hip with hers. His fingers tightened to steady her, and a slow ache of longing radiated from somewhere deep in her body. A new, completely different hurt made her aware of every part of her flesh.

She shivered uncontrollably. "Oh."

"I'm sorry," he said. "I have long legs."

"You have long legs," she echoed breathlessly, feeling more ridiculous than ever.

He peered down at her, arching one brow. "And you have nice legs. Don't think I hadn't noticed."

There was no way she could keep her mouth from curving into a smile. "I didn't say that as a compliment, Clifford. You don't have to return it in kind."

When she unwittingly used his Christian name, Clifford gradually slowed his pace. He marveled at the sudden disorganization of his lawyer's mind. He had stopped being a boy when he was fourteen years old. Now, sensations he thought were dead, or didn't even exist, spun crazily, madly inside his head.

She was wonderful! A delightful combination of woman-girl that reminded him of waltzes, dreamy drives in the moonlight and shared bites of an apple. She was a girl emerging into the true beauty of her womanhood; so much of her innocence existed it made him want to lift her off the ground and hold her tightly against his chest. He wanted to take her home to his family.

Sobering, he squinted against the wind flicking at his eyelashes. His family's hopes for his life were laid out—had been laid out for months—with painstaking care. Faith Chambers' place in it was deeply-rooted and scrupulously calculated. Personal satisfaction was something he hadn't believed existed, so their happiness was better than nothing.

Fool! he swore at himself. He was acting like a kid, stepping back from his life, devising ways to put this girl in it. Yet she hadn't even looked at him without anger simmering in those brown eyes.

Thirty-two years old was an awfully late age for a man to wake up and realize he has never been in love, or has never wanted something badly enough that he could die for it. Was that what he felt now? Was he exactly where he wanted to be, walking beside this woman who dropped papers and drove a jeep and made him taut with desire simply by looking at him?

He thought it was. God help him, he knew it was.

"You return what you like," he said gruffly, "and I'll return what I like."

"What?"

Their looks collided, each wearing surprise at how far away they had drifted into their own private musings.

Smiling, he shrugged his shoulders. "Nothing."

"Oh," she sighed and grasped the door of his car the moment he removed the key from the lock. From habit she opened the door herself.

At her unthinking display of independence, Clifford stepped out of the way. He watched, finding unexpected satisfaction in the unconscious beauty of her moves; such graceful, little things—a twist of her wrist, the nape of her neck.

If Victoria had glimpsed the undisguised hunger on Clifford's face, she would never have gotten in the car.

* * *

Victoria's first awareness of Clifford pulling the car to a stop was a fleeting impression of having been asleep. Yet she knew she had not. Where had she been? In another world? In another lifetime? Then she knew; she had been thinking about Faith Chambers. How, exactly, she wasn't certain. Yet, she suddenly suffered a sadness she couldn't comprehend. Somehow—with an instinct she was not familiar with—she knew Faith Chambers was in the right, and she was in the wrong.

Her anxious glance darted to Clifford as he switched off the engine. His masculinity was catlike as his legs stretched and strained against his jeans. He flexed his foot against the brake and the thick sinews shifted, the latent, masterful strength was capable of more power than she could ever possess. She understood why she was hurting.

Quickly she faced the solitude of the mist forming on her window. She sat here, looking at this man—*another woman's man*—and she wanted him as she had never wanted anyone in her life. And more than in a physical sense, because she craved to possess him, to be possessed by him, forever. She felt the hook now and knew, without any doubts, that she was falling in love.

Before this, she had always considered women who intruded into relationships to be bad women. It was such an inexcusable invasion. Women who did it deserved any retribution they got. And she was on the verge of doing it herself! She couldn't believe it!

The car had scarcely stopped when she groped distraughtly for the handle to the door. She wanted to get out of this car, away from Clifford Pennington. She didn't want to fall in love with him. She didn't want him to guess what she was thinking. She didn't want anyone to know the shameful step she had almost taken.

Fumbling with the door, she somehow managed to get it open. Before she could swing her feet to the ground Clifford caught the skirt of her coat.

"What's the matter?"

Victoria kept her head turned at an absurd angle. "I—"

Reaching across her, he jerked the door shut and imprisoned her with one precise click. "Look at me," he demanded. "What's the matter? What did I say this time?"

"You didn't say anything!" she cried.

He was forcibly turning her around, his hands heavy on her shoulders. She lifted the palms of her own hands as if she were shielding her head from a blow.

"Just don't . . ." she began hoarsely. "Don't . . ." In the eternal gesture of regret, Victoria closed her arms over her head, crushing the shimmering softness of her hair. Only then did she feel safe from those golden eyes which could see through her.

His gruffness came from deep in his chest, earnest and hoarse. "Don't do this," he pleaded. "Is it Brayntree? Is it the money? I told you I'd help you. I know it looks hopeless, but it's not. Believe me." He paused. *"Talk to me, dammit!"*

Talk to him? Tell him the mistake she had almost made? How she was the product of a life where she had worked like a machine, had made every minute count? That she didn't know men? That she didn't know how to handle herself in a situation like this?

Slumping back against the seat, breathing a long, disillusioned sigh, Victoria moistened her lips. "I can't explain it," she said in a quivering voice. "You wouldn't understand. Don't ask me any more questions. Just write down whatever you have to write down and let's get this thing done with. I have a school to run and I haven't done a very good job of it the last few days."

He disagreed. "I would understand."

He straightened his long body. Though she didn't look at him, she knew he gripped the wheel hard and frowned at some point dead ahead.

"No you wouldn't," she said.

Clifford made an incoherent sound deep in his throat. A space of time stretched out between them. Victoria's hand circled the strap to her handbag.

"Why do you say that?" he asked softly. "Because you know how much I want to hold you?"

Victoria thought, when she gaped at the determined angle of his jaw, that he would at least look at her. But he didn't. He hardly moved at all. He only touched the tips of his fingers to his moustache and stroked it as if he were sorting out a puzzle in his mind.

She waited, not knowing what to say.

"We're only postponing the inevitable," he continued after a rash disregard of his attorney's logic. "I will hold you, Victoria, and kiss you. You know that. And I'll make love to you because I want you so much it's breaking me. And it's hurting you, even if you lie and tell me it's not."

"No, Clifford—" she heard herself saying, though she meant to say it wasn't true.

"You can play games with your head if you want to," he went on, "but you know I'm right. For thirty-two years I've thought that something was wrong with me. Now it's happened. I'm damn sure not going to act like some school kid and throw it all away."

She struggled with her voice. She cleared her throat and tried to choke back a knot that felt as if it would strangle her.

"I have learned," she began in a squeaky, broken whimper. Swallowing hard, she attempted it again. "I have learned, just lately, since I buried my mother, that a person can make himself do most anything. I have also learned that feelings are not dependable."

"That is not completely true."

"Feelings," she declared in a determined tone which warned him to let her finish, "feelings change. And *that* is true. Right now I feel an unspeakable concern for a woman I don't even know, that I have no wish to know. I don't like that feeling, Clifford. It's even stronger than what I feel for you."

She became quiet, having inadvertently answered his question. Now he knew everything. Now she couldn't hide.

He dealt with her more gently than she imagined he would. He faced her honestly and this time she didn't look away. His eyes, when he moved them slowly, studying her hands, the white slope of her throat, the pinched set of her small jaw, were caressing.

"I won't ask you how you learned about Faith. It doesn't matter. She has nothing to do with what has happened between us."

"She exists, Clifford. She had the right to know how you spend your time. And that you're sitting in this car with me, telling me that you intend to make love to me. Oh, this is insane, Pennington! Please take me back."

Clifford deflected his palm off the steering wheel several times. They both looked at it to avoid looking at each other.

"I don't care how insane it is," he argued. "The relationship Faith and I have is not what you think."

"Not what I *think?* You're going to marry her! What am I supposed to think?"

His shoulders lifted with dissatisfaction. "Yes, but still—"

"People who plan to get married do things and say things. You have a relationship with her, for heaven's sake! You've probably made love to her, and you have the crazy nerve to tell me—"

"That something completely unplanned has happened in my life. I didn't know it, I didn't ask for it!" He twisted in his seat, the handsome planes of his face distorted with a confusion he was unused to. "Oh, hell! You tell me, Victoria. Tell me I'm making it up. Say to me that you don't want me to touch you. Right now, this minute."

"I want to go back to my car."

"Will you walk with me?"

"Yes."

They walked for nearly an hour. Clifford had parked beside a little wooded knoll which spread behind the construction site of a two-block cluster of new homes. The grassy meadow was serving as a park for several neighborhoods before it, too, surrendered to progress. Before the bulldozers and sidewalks claimed it, it was polka-dotted with a see-saw and a slide and bicycle paths. Around a bend, at the foot of a tumbling slope, the wind rippled a finely populated duckpond.

Only valiant, brave souls lingered this late on such a chilly evening. The skies threatened to deluge the land. Old women took one last walk before going home to small rooms and a television. Several noisy children took enormous pleasure in chasing the

ducks. As Victoria and Clifford discussed—
sometimes quite heatedly—the pros and cons of a
private loan, the last stooped old woman gathered
up her shopping bag from the five-and-ten and
shuffled to the bus stop three blocks away.

Victoria's brown eyes narrowed austerely as she
told him that Ed Barnes's figure of two hundred
thousand dollars was preposterous. How could she
complain? he came back; it only made her worth
that much more. That was all well and good for him
to take such a view, she lashed out; he didn't face the
prospects of trying to make ends meet and pay back
such a staggering amount. She simply must re-assess
her opportunities for income. Perhaps there were
avenues she had overlooked, he suggested with a
patience she guessed he was enjoying.

"I know what my potentials are," she snapped and
yanked at the belt of her coat. "I've been managing
without you for the first twenty-two years of my life,
Pennington."

Clifford coughed a short laugh. "I rest my case."

The infection of his laughter was contagious. She
noticed the way his hair tended to curl about his ears
in the dampness. And his jaw was sprouting the faint
stubble of a shadowy beard. He wasn't nearly as
ferocious as he sounded and she giggled, pausing in
her step.

"Oh, Pennington, I should have hit you back that
very first day."

He looked over his shoulder at her laughing,
upturned face. "Go ahead," he challenged.

"Go ahead, *what*?"

"Take your punch," he said and swung his body a
half turn so that they faced each other. "You've got
one coming."

Victoria raked him with teasing, dancing eyes. From the distance drifted the contented quacking and squawking of the ducks. The temptation to romp happened as naturally as the drizzle which glistened on their cheeks.

She aimed a clenched fist at the center of his jacket, but before she could bury it in that vital spot Clifford's fingers circled firmly about her wrist. She pushed and they tightened their masterful grip. She heard the deep rumble of his mirth.

Swiftly caught up in the minor skirmish, Victoria pushed earnestly. But he only held her more securely at bay. Before she realized it, she was strenuously resisting him, chewing at her lower lip as intently as a man when he is locked in the throes of an arm wrestle.

"Ohhh, you!" she groaned finally and crumpled into a delightful and charming bundle of wilted womanpower. "That's not fair, you beast!"

He chuckled softly. "It's a man's prerogative to cheat."

Something about the poignant edge of his facetious retort sobered Victoria. Lifting her face, she blinked back the raindrops which sparkled on her forehead and the tip of her nose like broken diamonds. Oh, Lord, she thought, it was happening again. Wasn't there anything this man could do that didn't stir that awful ache inside her?

His depth of intimacy seemed impossible. She stood unmoving as he studied her parted lips. Gradually his fingers loosened their tenacious grip on her hand, but they didn't release it. His fingertips slipped higher up her wrist in a search for the warm throb of her pulse.

Breathless, she waited as if for some ominous verdict which would condemn her. Then she felt her own heartbeat surging against his fingers, flowing from her body into his.

His glance pierced her sharply. "A little rapid, I think," he diagnosed with his gentle drawl.

The situation was already out of hand. She thrashed about in her mind for anything to say. She must, in her woman's wisdom, think of some tactful way to get herself back home—safe to Brayntree, safe from this spell which beguiled her into doing and saying things she didn't intend to.

She fished aimlessly in her coat pocket for a crumpled package of cheese crackers which she had discovered under the seat of the jeep over a week ago. Holding it up as if it were an unexpected treasure, she opened her mouth to speak and didn't say anything.

"Hungry?" he asked, grinning.

"No, not for me," she protested. "For . . ." her breath persisted in catching, "for the ducks. I mean, I'd like to feed the ducks."

"I adore ducks," he said and glanced up at the raindrops which were growing larger. "But we're going to get caught in the rain. Come on."

Grasping her hand as a thick gray pall descended between them and the Porsche sitting nearly two blocks away, Clifford ran with her toward a stand of trees nearly obscured by undergrowth. It was a thickly tangled mass of oak trees and several seasons of prolific, untended honeysuckle vines. A few leaves still clung despite the early frost of winter, and they rambled over the neglected remains of an ancient gazebo. Nearly dragging her up the rickety steps, he ducked his head beneath the low rafters and hauled them both into the dry haven.

"I want to feed the ducks," he mimicked and sloughed the water off her coat with a touch which

would have been indecent under other circumstances.

Victoria blotted at her gleaming cheeks with the
tips of her fingers and pretended she wasn't shaking
from being handled so. "It won't last long," she said
optimistically.

"Blind faith." He stamped his feet to shed the
water.

Stooping to rue the sogginess of her shoes, she
found herself straightening in slow motion. She
knew, as she drew herself upward, what would
happen. As surely as if they had been progressing to
this point all their lives, she knew he would kiss her.
But knowing didn't lessen her reluctance. She had
never really believed the slogan of her own generation: If it feels good, do it. So when Clifford made
that mysterious movement to take her in his arms,
she drew back.

"Oh, Pennington," she whispered and leaned far
away from him and crossed her arms over her
breasts.

He said nothing. He only flexed his elbow and
drew her close into the curve of his body as thunder
rumbled in the distance and rain drummed a frenzied staccato upon the tin of the roof.

When Victoria felt the muscular vibrancy of his
body against hers, she thought, *This man is going to
kiss me. I don't dare close my eyes. Please, Clifford,
don't make me like it.*

"I don't want to hurt anyone." She shaped her lips
about the words, meaning them, yet she wasn't
certain if he understood that she was talking about
Faith.

Clifford's head bent anyway, and she watched it
gradually fill her vision until there was nothing but
him: the narrow plane of his nose, the whisper of his

breathing, the smell of him, the crisp brush of his moustache against the hollow of her cheek.

With genuine shock she realized the man was as shaken as she. He was brilliant, much more worldly-wise than she, yet, as his hands urged her own fingers loose, freeing their knotted lacing, he was trembling. His breath, when he lifted her hands to rest limply upon his shoulders, tore raggedly. Then his head dipped, cautiously at first. His mouth found the dewy corner of hers and brushed it in a delicate wisp of a kiss, as if he were making one last plea for her to stop him from violating a commitment he had sworn long ago to someone else.

Victoria didn't struggle when Clifford moved his tongue inside her mouth to learn about such a personal part of her, tasting, experimenting, reaching deeper and deeper until she accepted him and her mouth seemed more his than hers. Her breasts surged, came alive, throbbing with a primitive need for him to touch them. Yet he did not. Some insane part of her mind became aware of him unbuttoning her coat. She inanely counted the buttons and felt her belt falling loose at her sides.

The rain deafened them. It was such an easy thing to let her eyes flutter closed, to drop her head back against the possessive circle of his arm and let him crush her against his chest. For this one moment she would forget that his touch was not forever.

Clifford's hand moved beneath her coat and smoothed the lines of her back. Inch by inch he traced her spine, then dropped lower to explore the gentle slope of her hips. The discreet film of her slip shifted below her skirt. He groaned. Burying his fingers into the soft, sweet cushion of her buttocks, he lifted her upward against him. The demands of his own man's need stirred, bold and urgent.

Instinctively Victoria strained to touch her toes to the floor and in doing so pressed even nearer to his ready passion.

"Please," he murmured into her mouth. "Let me love you, sweetheart. Really love you. Let me, let me."

Never could she admit how his desire enflamed her. Yet she couldn't keep from showing him. She slanted her lips beneath his. The danger of the hook went deep now, as real as the irresistible scent of him filling her nostrils. He could hurt her; he could kill her.

"Kiss me," she begged, "but don't ask me that."

A crazy, disoriented mixture of sensations rushed at her from all directions and she had only a hazy impression of the passing time. She drifted inside his mind, inside his bones. Nothing was real until presently she grew cognizant of the gradual lessening of the rain.

Once more cautious, she pushed herself from him. "I hope you don't get the wrong idea," she managed to say in a ragged breath.

Clifford settled her firmly onto the floor and drew her head down to his shoulder. The sound of his quiet, contented groan didn't settle her composure at all. With the lightest of gestures, he arranged the moist tresses of her hair into a semblance of order beneath his chin.

"I get only the ideas you give me, little cricket," he muttered, "and if you don't know what they are, I will make you a list."

"No. I mean, I do know what I did. I'm not *that* . . . well, I just don't want you to get the mistaken impression . . . that I would do it again. Or that it means anything."

"Oh," he said after a time, as if he had thought it over carefully and didn't accept a word of it.

After a moment Victoria smiled at his odd little term of affection. "Clifford?"

"What?"

"Do you know what crickets do?" she asked against the hard pillow of his chest.

"Chirp."

She hissed a scolding sound. "Besides that! I saw one once. He flipped over on his back and squiggled down in the dirt and rested a few minutes with his feet straight up in the air. After a little while, as happily as you please, he flipped over and hopped away."

Clifford tossed back his head and laughed. It was the first time she had seen him freely, thoroughly happy. Then, simply because he was happy, she leaned back against his hands which were locked behind her back and laughed, too.

His look adored her. "How do you know it was a 'he'?"

"Because he was arrogant!"

"That wasn't arrogance," he argued, grinning. "He was actually in the throes of death because of some faithless female. It suddenly came to him what a waste it was and he decided to give life another go."

"It was arrogance," she sniffed, then cut her eyes coquettishly. "I have a grasshopper story."

Clifford rolled his eyes upward. "My luck to have taken up with a bug freak."

"Hush! It's a true story." Her brows drew together. "Like the other one."

Sighing, he said with pretended indulgence, "Go on."

Victoria relaxed against the support of his hands at her back. "This grasshopper crashed into my windshield headfirst, you see. It knocked him as cold as a . . ."

"Cucumber," Clifford supplied gravely.

"Thank you. Anyway, he lay there on the hood, at sixty miles an hour, for about a minute. When he came to he had an awful headache. I could tell by the groggy way he finally straggled up to the windshield's wiper blade. He hooked his little feet about it and hung on for dear life until I finally stopped."

"What did he do then, madam, say 'thank you for the ride'?"

Her brown eyes narrowed playfully. "You don't believe me."

Laughing, Clifford rotated her in the circle of his arm. "I believe you, I believe you," he said and tucked his chin to peer at the buttons of her blouse. With the tip of one finger he nudged the top one lazily. It pulled free, and Victoria lowered her eyes to see the pale curve of her breast between them. His knuckle bent as he drew it along the rounded swell.

Gasping, realizing that if things got out of hand again she wouldn't be able to even walk away from this place, Victoria used the oldest ploy known to man. She teased. Laughing, she clutched her blouse shut and whirled away from him. "You men are all alike. Cricket or grasshopper, you never quit."

His mouth pursed thoughtfully and he didn't protest when the moment ended so decidedly. He didn't try to prevent her from leaving him to peer out at the weather. He squinted at the Porsche, too.

"We'd better make the most of this slack while it lasts," he suggested.

Victoria nodded wordlessly and followed him down the steps. She craved some time alone now, to lie down and try to understand what had happened to her, what it meant. Would it be so terribly wrong, she wondered, to take him from Faith if she could? Would Faith Chambers, whoever she was, play fair with her if the roles were reversed?

Once Victoria climbed into the car beside Clifford she leaned back in her seat and almost grew at ease with him. She drowsily watched the buildings flitting past her window. She expected him to turn off Gloucester Street onto Boundary, to the familiar triangle occupied by William and Mary College where, she hoped, her jeep was still parked.

But instead of passing the vine-covered President's House and the Wren Building, the Porsche rumbled down some of Williamsburg's streets where two centuries could be seen living peacefully, side by side. They drove past Market Square and continued further where Francis Street became York Road.

"But my car," she protested, sitting up when she realized he wasn't just taking the long way back as a devious play for time.

"Later," he said and flicked on the turn signal.

For a moment she sat gaping at the tiny flashing warning. *Be careful*, it ticked. *Be careful.*

"No, not later." She reached out her hand as if she would place it over his on the steering wheel.

"Uh-huh," he said and braked the great, pulsing piece of machinery. They paused, the engine idling.

"Where are we?"

Wrenching her head about, she saw a long, winding drive lined on both sides with dogwood trees bare of leaves. Beyond it was a two-story home with two chimneys, one towering at each end. The center doorway was porticoed, and the added wings which extended out from each side had their own doors and porticos. The gardens were extensive and formally tended. Even from where she sat she recognized one of history's grand old mansions in a restored state of upkeep.

"This'll only take a moment," he told her, looking pleased. "I need to get some things for you from my office here at home."

A disturbing sense of disaster seeped through Victoria. She shook her head from side to side. This was the last thing she had expected from him.

"Well," she declared firmly, "please hurry. I'll wait for you in the car."

Clifford frowned, assuming the disagreeable look she was acquainted with by now. The sting of it made her flinch. "I'll be damned if you will," he growled.

The car shot down the drive and came to a skidding stop beside two other cars. "Ah, Devon's home."

In that one second she could have slapped his face. Her entire dishabille unnerved her, and she fluffed at her hair. "I look awful."

"You look fine. We'll be right in and right out."

Her brown eyes hardened with resolve. "Clifford Pennington, you must be deaf. I told you I wouldn't go in. Who do you think you are, bringing me here without even telling me what you were doing? You may do that with other people, but not with me!"

He flicked off the key and, as if he hadn't heard a word she said, got out of the car and limberly dodged the fresh puddles of rainwater to open her door. Beneath the moustache his grin flashed light-heartedly.

Cursing him under her breath, Victoria acknowledged he had placed her neatly in check. If anyone spied her sitting in the car she would look as suspicious as a criminal's accomplice. Or even worse (she recalled Belle Watling waiting in her carriage in *Gone with the Wind*) like some nineteenth century *demimonde* whose reputation would not be tolerated in the house.

Angrily she twisted herself up and out of the car. "This is outrageous," she said through gritted teeth.

"You're right, it is."

"I hope your glib tongue can lie its way around the way we look, coming in here like a couple of half-drowned pups. Never in my life have I felt so . . . so . . ."

"Desirable," he interjected. "Like nothing I've ever known before in my life."

Her foot went slamming into the edge of the sidewalk. Clifford, catching her by a conveniently outflung arm, stopped in his tracks and peered down at her as if he were anywhere else except in front of his own home.

His nose, she thought madly, was almost too pretty to be a man's nose. It was fashioned like a sculptor would shape it, straight, narrow, in two skillful strokes. *What was she doing standing on his sidewalk daydreaming like a ninny?*

"Yes," he drawled, knowing she had been studying him, "and I like you, too."

He still held her arm, and she snatched it free. "Don't do that!"

Devilment crinkled the lines about his eyes. "But you're such a clumsy little cricket, Victoria. I never know if you're going to fall at my feet."

She couldn't resist the temptation to snap up his

baited hook. "I don't know why I even trusted you in the first place, Pennington! You bring out the absolute worst in me."

She thought he retorted, "I only hope to live so long." But her cheeks flamed a perfect scarlet, and she didn't dare ask him to repeat it.

Still chuckling and choosing to ignore the defiant thrust of her jaw, Clifford ushered Victoria along the shrub-lined sidewalk with the same easy skill that he had maneuvered her into his classroom against her will. Pushing open the front door, he nudged her forward into a long, high-ceilinged corridor lighted by a chandelier whose value she wouldn't have attempted to estimate.

Many of Williamsburg's cherished old homes had been sold with the restriction that the owner must possess the property for life. Any following owner was assigned on lease. In that manner, the restoration of the city was passed from hand to hand. Virginia's youth and dashing cavalier days were preserved. The history of the splendid years when Williamsburg was a center of government and the hub of a gay social whirl was captured in these elegant restored homes.

Preserving tradition was Victoria's weakness anyway. It had forced her to fight for her own Brayntree. Now the familiar sense of stepping back to an earlier century carried her away. Awed, she felt the error of her presence even more.

A woman's low, musical voice called from another room nearby. "Is that you, Clifford? Faith and I have been looking all over town for you."

Victoria came face to face with Clifford's mother. Her first thought was that the words "I have been kissing your betrothed son" had to be flashing across her forehead in bright, garish neon. Her feet were rooted into the floor and refused to move forward.

Madeline Pennington, a woman in her late fifties, was one of the most elegant women Victoria had ever seen. Her beauty touched the silver of her hair, the gracious gestures of her hands, the eloquent subtleties in her carriage. It was an ageless kind of loveliness which had little to do with clothes or clever makeup, a slightly haunting beauty, wistful.

Her perfectly arched brows lifted in surprise at finding a strange woman in the hallway. "Oh," she said kindly. "Please do come in."

Bending his dark head, Clifford gently kissed his mother's cheek. Victoria's memories of kissing her own mother were too painfully close for her to watch this scene. For the second time in one day the tall man's tenderness dumbfounded her. His manner —particularly his softened words—reminded her of a young boy who draws a treasured possession to his chest, fearful that something will hurt it.

"I'm sorry I'm late," he said and casually motioned Victoria forward. "Mother, this is Miss Carroll. We need to get some things from the office. Faith's here, you say?"

Victoria despised the warm color she knew was diffusing on her neck and over her cheeks. She had never felt more out of place in her life, nor more desperate to escape.

"I'm intruding," she apologized flatly. "Mr. Pennington, I can do this another time. It isn't even necessary to take me back to the college. I can—"

A tiny muscle leaped angrily in Clifford's jaw, though his words came without the slightest hesitation and were ridiculously polite. "I've delayed this young woman shamelessly, Mother," he confessed. "I hope we can at least offer her a cup of coffee. Didn't Dad go to Richmond?"

"Not until tomorrow," Madeline said as she smiled at Victoria. "I'm being rude. Miss Carroll, do stay for a moment." Before Victoria could respond the woman slipped her arm through Clifford's as if the matter were settled. "I was beginning to worry, darling. Ed Barnes drove Faith and me out to look at the house. The more I see it, Cliff, the more perfect it seems to me. I can hardly wait until you two buy it. There are so many things I want to do."

"Mother—"

"We picked up some wallpaper samples. But we wanted you to be the one to choose, of course."

All during Madeline's enthusiastic account of the afternoon, they neared the living room. As Victoria mumbled a hoarse protest which she was sure no one heard, they all stepped through an open door. Victoria carefully kept her mouth in a tight little smile and thought this had to be the most atrociously awkward moment of her entire life. How could Clifford dare to force her into his life like this? She being the extra woman with whom no one would know what to do.

"I will never forgive you for this," she whispered as he drew her past him with a meaningful pressure of his hand at the small of her back.

The room was actually two combined drawing rooms—immense, beautiful, lived-in and decorated with a superb taste that didn't surprise her. She received a number of impressions at once. A fire crackled cheerfully and mingled its gracious scent with that of fresh flowers. Two men rose and the younger woman glided across the room toward Clifford.

Victoria's heartbeat plummeted miserably to her feet. Faith was indeed beautiful! In fact the most feminine thing she had ever seen, with shimmering blond hair falling over her shoulders in a sensual, windblown effect. Her Dresden complexion was so carefully made up she resembled a photographer's color plate out of Glamour Magazine.

But her most winsome characteristic was her vulnerability. Victoria could imagine most any man wishing instantly to protect her. She could never picture Faith Chambers wearing knee-high rubber boots and jeans, bailing out buckets of water from a flooded basement as she and Stephanie had done more than once. She wouldn't drop things or get caught in the rain and kiss someone else's fiancé under a dilapidated gazebo either. She would be the perfect wife for Clifford!

Praying her smile remained intact long enough to survive this encounter, Victoria barely heard Clifford's nimble explanation about how they had gotten caught in a rainstorm. She didn't care! she told herself. She didn't care if he kissed Faith. He could kiss her a thousand times, and she wouldn't care. *She wanted out of here!*

". . . did you, Miss Carroll?"

"What?" Victoria blinked. Her fingers fluttered to her throat. "I—"

"You remember the property settlement, Dad," Clifford rescued her as he refreshed his father's memory. "The plaintiff is a temporary resident of Austria."

"Oh, yes." Ethan Pennington stepped forward and took Victoria's fingers with courteous, old-fashioned gallantry. "Now I remember. And this is the lovely defendant. I believe I knew your mother, Miss Carroll."

Victoria brightened a fraction. Ethan Pennington resembled his older son much more than the younger. He was somewhat heavier than Clifford, and his sideburns were snowy white. His jaw wasn't quite so angular. Yet the same character penetrated his facial features: strong, aggressive, not easily deceived.

"Are you sure all this is legal, Cliff?"

From the older, graying version of Clifford, Victoria's eyes darted to the younger, ruddy version. Devon Pennington pulled himself away from the wall where he had been observing everything. An attractive boyish grin, minus the frame of the moustache, revealed his approval of her. Quite slender and sandy-haired, he seemed to be a habitually contented man.

"What d'you mean?" Clifford lowered his lanky frame onto a winged chair by the fireplace, slumping on his spine and propping one ankle across a knee. Faith perched lightly on its arm and crossed her long, willowy legs to perfect advantage.

"I mean," Devon replied, reaching out his hand as if to take Victoria's coat which she was absently unbuttoning, "is it legal to be on good terms with both the plaintiff and the defendant?"

Clifford grimaced comically. "As long as someone's case isn't damaged, klutz."

Devon accepted her leather coat and folded it neatly on the back of a nearby chair. "Ah, then we forgive you for being late. Miss Carroll, you will stay for coffee, won't you? You must, or I'll dash out into the street and throw myself in front of a car in protest."

Unaware that her lips parted, Victoria stood staring at the younger Pennington replica. He was probably three years older than she was. The warmth in his eyes told her more than his laughing words. *Everything is all right,* they said. *Don't let this family overwhelm you.*

"Then I guess I must stay," she agreed breathlessly. "I don't want to be responsible for your early demise."

"Exactly." He motioned her to a chair beside his, then inched his even nearer.

Madeline Pennington glided regally to the door. "I'll be in the kitchen."

"I'll come with you," Faith volunteered.

What had she been thinking? Victoria wondered as the two women left the room with their heads bent in the way of close friends when they share gossip. Had Victoria hoped that Faith was a scheming, hateful witch so she could hate her on sight? She tried not to watch them. She pretended to find fault with the stitching on the toe of her beige shoe, but a great wave of loneliness for her own mother washed over her.

During the next half hour the tedium of exchanging civilities taxed Victoria to the limit. Her usually quick tongue seemed capable of only the most sluggish monosyllables. When the women returned, she balanced a china cup in the palm of her hand with the same poise she had repetitously drilled into her girls. She smiled and answered dozens of questions about Brayntree's history and pretended to be elated when she shared a couple of hilarious anecdotes about emergencies which were anything but hilarious when they had happened. All the while she tried not to notice Clifford's long brown fingers as they rested loosely upon Faith's knee, nor Faith's arm across the back of his chair, the graceful curve of her breast outlined only inches from his jaw.

"There're really only three wall coverings to choose from, Clifford," Madeline was saying as she deposited a large open book of sample wall coverings into her older son's lap. Faith bent lower, pointing, her hand occasionally touching Clifford's, her dazzling hair cascading about her cheeks, a strand lingering on his cheek which he absently brushed aside.

Over Clifford's head Madeline conversed with her husband. "It reminds me when we started work on this place, Ethan," she declared, cheerful, elated. The brightness sparkling in her eyes seemed a bit too gay, Victoria thought, as if Madeline were trying terribly hard to be happy. Ethan's love for his wife was profound and obvious to anyone who cared to look for it. Stepping to her side, he slipped an arm about her waist and smiled, not at the samples, but at her.

Disheartened as she swallowed down the hollow emptiness, for a moment Victoria almost hated Clifford for allowing her to even see what a real family was like. She had never really known. Now that she saw the camaraderie, the playful bantering and bickering, the cheerful insults, she miserably wished she had remained ignorant.

An intense need to cry knotted in her throat. She dropped her eyes to her lap and battled to keep the smile on her lips, despite the fact that her eyes blurred.

Even though they were separated by a large room and a number of jousting opinions, she instantly knew when Clifford's eyes were on her. She also knew that if she looked at him, her starving loneliness would be painted on her face. She couldn't bear for him to see it, but neither could she prevent her brown eyes from lifting.

His probing scrutiny was a poignant communication that couldn't have lasted more than four or five seconds. He told her he wanted her to understand. She informed him she wished she were anywhere but here.

"The one that really concerns me, darling," Faith said as Clifford resumed his task, "is for the old ballroom. Do you like the Chinese theme? The curtains could be yellow silk, and the chandelier could be shipped from Canton in a couple of months at the most."

"Tell us, Miss Carroll," Devon urged softly.

Caught off guard, Victoria started.

He leaned over the back of her own chair with an attentiveness which bordered on teasing, perhaps even flirtation. A deep line creased the space between Clifford's brows when his brother spoke. Victoria was aware of it as sharply as a well-placed kick on her shin. Clifford was a chauvanist!

Impulsively she dazzled Devon with a smile and hoped Clifford saw it. "Tell you what?" she asked sweetly.

He smiled. "When it's all said and done, wouldn't you trade all those Brayntree girls for a house full of boys? Once in a while you would, wouldn't you? Come on, the truth."

Laughing softly, Victoria pressed the corner of a starched napkin to her lips. She didn't answer in a loud voice, and even though Clifford leaned his head to hear Faith's murmured remark, she was certain the older brother missed nothing of what was going on across the room.

"Well," she confessed, including Ethan Pennington in the conversation, "when it's good, it's really good. When it's bad?" She lifted her slender shoulders in a charming motion that left her attitude in doubt. "Girls have their little ways of tormenting a person. I guess I'll have to admit that they're more difficult to deal with than boys."

"I disagree." Madeline's cup and saucer clattered to the carpet with a startling tinkle of fine glass against glass.

Ethan Pennington leaped to his feet.

Devon's breath made a harsh, grating sound.

A pale circle of brown coffee spread on the carpet as if offering some sad, mysterious commentary. Before anyone could reach Madeline, Faith knelt gently beside the older woman, blotting at the stain with her napkin and murmuring that it was nothing, nothing at all.

It was a tense tableau: Ethan bending over his wife, the distressed angle of Madeline's head which distorted the beautiful features, the slow-motion reaction of the two sons as if they debated the wisdom of becoming involved.

Victoria stiffened with anxiety. What had she said?

Madeline whispered in a small child's plea for help. "Ethan?"

"It's all right, darling," Ethan comforted his wife, glancing over her head at Victoria. He was a man who was impeccably groomed and who enjoyed a measure of success most would never know. Yet, at this moment, he appeared utterly helpless. He sent a mute apology across the room, and Victoria wasn't certain why.

More disturbing than Ethan was the unexpected apathy of Clifford. He sat unmoving, his legs crossed, a slightly defeated droop to his shoulders, one hand covering his mouth as he stared blindly at the scene.

"Shh," Ethan urged his wife to regain her composure. "It's only a cup. Let me take you to your room, dearest."

"But I'm always doing stupid things like that," she mourned in a raspy whisper.

"Miss Carroll," Ethan inclined his silvering head to her, "we're so glad you stopped by. Please come any time. You'll excuse us now, won't you?"

"Of course," Victoria mumbled, praying she would never have to set foot in this house again. Her hands had lost all feeling by the time she realized she was wringing them mercilessly. What was she witnessing? Something was badly wrong here, but what?

As if he read her troubled thoughts, Devon dropped on one knee to the carpet beside her foot. He didn't look at her but plucked at a thread as his parents left the room. "It was my fault," he said. "I just didn't think."

"But I—" Victoria interrupted. She couldn't shake off a feeling of horror. Yet she clamped her jaw and didn't try to explain further.

Not caring how rude she looked, she suddenly jumped to her feet and began pulling on her coat and buttoning it. "I really must go. I can get the names another time, Mr. Pennington."

Faith was methodically straightening the mess and began collecting stray cups and saucers around the room. If she thought anything was amiss, she kept her face discretely serene and all traces of irritation hidden.

"No!" Clifford's emphasis sliced through the murky tension. He paused, then spoke with a low, precise control. "There's no need for that. I'll get them for you now."

Their familiar mode of communication was static like a ragged electrical current. The impact of it

drained the strength from her, and she unknowingly
groped behind herself for the support of a chair. It
seemed impossible that Faith or Devon would miss
reading the disturbed messages.

Devon apparently understood since he immediately answered his brother's look. "I'll take her
home, Cliff."

Victoria's palm turned upward in objection. "Oh,
please," she begged. "No trouble. Really."

Smiling at them both, Devon assured Victoria,
"It's no trouble."

"I need a way home myself, Cliff," Faith interjected. "Daddy brought me by and dropped me off
because I was sure you'd come straight from the
college. You don't mind, do you?"

Clifford's pause was a hair's breadth, infinitely
hard to detect. "Of course," he replied pleasantly.
"Gather up all your samples, dear. I'm afraid I
wasn't much help, was I?"

When Faith told him sweetly that it didn't matter,
Victoria wanted to scream at Clifford. He had no
right to make her watch this. It was inhumane,
heartless. She didn't want to see anything through
Faith's eyes. She didn't want to understand what the
other woman felt. Was it because she saw, as Faith
did, Clifford's odd, unexplainable vulnerability?
Was she falling so in love with Clifford herself that
she was damned to suffer for it? No. No!

"No," she breathed and was shocked to hear the
unexpected sound of her own voice.

She knew she was behaving badly. At this point
she didn't care. When Devon touched her elbow
with cautious, urging fingers, drawing her nearer the
sheerly draped windows, it didn't occur to her to
refuse to follow him. His kind of intimacy seemed

completely appropriate, like words of pity to someone who is dying.

"It's no big mystery, Miss Carroll," he explained
as if they had all the time in the world. He searched
to meet her eyes. Finally, out of politeness, she
smiled stiffly. "This has all made you feel ill at ease,"
he said. "Please don't. Sometimes certain things
strike Mother, and she breaks down for a moment.
You see, Cliff and I once had a sister, an older
sister."

The drapery crumpled in his tight fist, and Victoria stared at the white knuckles.

"Oh?"

"It's been a year now," he said. "It was one of
those long, drawn-out deaths that nearly killed
Mother, too. There are times when no one can get
her out of those depressions except Faith."

"Faith?" Victoria's mouth mimed the name as her
mind grappled with the grievous, unchangable facts.

Together they glanced back at Faith as she smiled
at Clifford. The disorder of the spill was repaired,
and they stood in the doorway to the hall, talking.
Clifford had removed his sport jacket, and it draped
across his shoulder by the hook of a crooked finger,
leisurely and unaffected.

"Yes, he is," remarked Devon, and Victoria
wrenched her face away. Smiling was impossible.
She didn't even exert herself to pretend. They
weren't talking about Madeline Pennington anymore, or her grief.

"Who is what?" Victoria choked, needing to hear
him say it.

Devon shrugged the simple way one brother does
about another brother. "Cliff's what every woman
looks for—good looking, eloquent, gets a lot of

flashy results at what he does for a living. Me? I'm an
archeologist. All I generally get is these." He held
up two hands whose palms were crusty with the
buildup of callouses. With the tip of one questing
finger, he touched the cuff of Victoria's coat as if he
were saying *Listen closely to what I'm not telling you,
Victoria.*

Victoria sniffed and tried not to notice Clifford's
trim waist, the firm lean buttocks upon which the
patch pockets of his jeans outlined his wallet and the
slight bulge of a crumpled handkerchief. "There's
nothing wrong with being an archeologist," she said
dully. "Quite the opposite."

"Faith and Lisa were very close," Devon continued, making his point as if she hadn't spoken. "Like
sisters, you understand. Faith literally grew up in this
house. She was another kid around. After Lisa died,
since she and Faith were the same age, something in
Mother's grief just . . . well, hung on to Faith."

Vague things shifted in Victoria's mind. She felt as
if she were straining to see objects underwater. Her
head bent forward in the gesture of submission, and
her waves fell demurely about her cheeks.

"This marriage means everything to Mother," he
finished soberly.

Then she knew. Then she understood what Devon
wasn't saying. Though the silence shattered her with
its shrieking noises of protest, she understood. To lie
to Devon, when he had risked exposure to tell her
such a private thing, would be wrong. She wouldn't
insult him by pretending she didn't realize Clifford
was marrying Faith because of his mother. A woman
could fight another woman for the man she loved,
but not something so complex as a mother's delicate
grief.

"How could you tell?" she mumbled, her head still bent. "About me, I mean?"

"It wasn't too hard. Maybe I'm used to watching for it. Perhaps something deep inside me resents it always happening to him." He coughed lightly and smiled. Victoria got the impression he wished to shield her from a danger only he could see. "Cliff would hurt everyone—Faith, especially himself—to protect Mother. He watched her nearly die. You should . . . well, you should just protect yourself."

Of their own accord, Victoria's eyes closed; she simply couldn't face any more truths today. A devastating weariness seeped through her bones, and she wished she were home, safe at Brayntree. Where would she ever find the strength to get home?

"I need to go," she said and gave Devon a sad, understanding smile.

Devon smiled back. "Life isn't always a nice row of pretty little boxes, is it?"

She was unable to thank him for fear of weeping. From across the room she sensed Clifford fastening his gaze on her. He motioned for her to follow him.

"This won't take but a minute, Devon," he said and moved toward the hall.

Like some creaking, wind-up doll, Victoria obeyed his summons. She forced her feet to step forward even though she wanted to walk out of the house. Any fairytale notions she had cherished about coming between Clifford and Faith were dashed now, even if she could have actually done it. Madeline Pennington had innocently placed handcuffs on her older son, and he would never tell her so.

She felt she was dying by slow, torturous degrees.

Chapter Five

As the door of Clifford's office crashed open, Victoria swallowed her anguish. Her offended speech of "how-could-you-do-this-to-me?" knotted in her throat. Even though she had rehearsed it behind his back every foot of the long, twisting corridor.

If she informed Clifford of how defeated she felt when Faith sat on the arm of his chair, she would expose her own self. Her jealousy had mushroomed into a jaded green suspicion, and it was ugly and repugnant to her. So, she bit her lips until they were numb and said nothing.

Clifford's steps into the room were uneven and ready for a battle, she guessed. The light was turned on and flooded the masculine room. She gazed at a wide expanse of carpet and drapes in warm, earthy hues, furniture covered in velvet and expensive leather. Doors opened off the office to his private apartment with its own porticoed entrance and telephone system. The only clashing contradiction in the mellow, old-world decor was a gleaming set of weights which monopolized one corner. That explained Clifford's flat stomach and hard, elastic muscles.

With the toe of his shoe Clifford kicked the door shut. Now Victoria became more aware of the bronzed skin stretched tightly across his cheekbones and the creases about his eyes which deepened with determination. Her own stance in the center of the room radiated defiance as powerful and as unrelenting as his.

The click of the door shutting echoed through the quiet like the threatening hammer of a revolver being pulled back. Adamant, Victoria swept past him. She snatched the door open with a dramatic Scarlett O'Hara flair, countering his statement with one of her own.

"Spare me the lecture," Clifford ordered gruffly, reading her message when she faced him again. "I didn't arrange any of this. I had no idea Faith would be here."

The room, even the way Clifford fit into it, dwarfed her. When he took three steps nearer she felt as if she were being backed into a trap by a stealthy wolf on the hunt. Her voice shook when she said, "You don't owe me any explanations. You don't owe me anything."

Clifford's oath rippled, blistering with ire. His mouth twisted sensually downward, and his body, when he shifted it, moved nearer still.

Wincing, Victoria threw out one hand to stop him. "Don't you dare touch me. I mean it. Not after that . . . display in there."

A whispering movement behind her startled her. She turned to see an ink-black cat walking through Clifford's door with dainty majesty. Unperturbed by their tempers, he crossed the carpet and rubbed against her legs with a loud, friendly purr. It seemed so ironically out of place that she nearly giggled.

Scooping up the aloof animal, who, though he didn't resent it, didn't appear overly excited, Victoria cuddled the large tomcat to her bosom like a battle-shield.

"Don't touch me," she repeated more firmly.

She had no idea of the admiration Clifford had for her as he watched her bend to lift the cat. Her fine coppery head should never have to bow to anything, he thought, least of all his more dominant physical power. His plea was husky with remorse for having placed her at such a disadvantage.

"Victoria, listen to me."

"I listened to you before, and now I'm miserable. Give me the names. Or don't give them to me, I don't care anymore. I just want to go back to Brayntree."

For a moment she expected that he would at least explain how wrong he was, or tell her his engagement to Faith was a charade for his mother's sake, or how much he would like to get out of it, or that he would like to do *some*thing to make things better.

"You're a little idiot," he said at last and stepped to throw back the top to the old-fashioned desk. It clattered loudly. Clifford, she decided, had an aversion to explaining himself, as if it were a weakness.

He withdrew a sheet of crisp white paper. Tossing it to the surface of the desk with the heedless detachment of a man whose thoughts are locked upon an extremely disagreeable subject, he heaved a long sigh.

Resenting his whole attitude, Victoria made an unwise choice of words. She lifted her chin and said:

"And Stephanie was right about you, Clifford. You really are a bastard."

For one split second his eyes slashed her like golden razors. Then he smirked. "That's me," he agreed sarcastically. He threw down the pen he had been twirling in his fingers. "I'm rotten to the core. I seduce young virgins all the time. Lurk behind old buildings and take great delight every time I make one cry."

"Oh, hush up, Pennington!" she cried and hugged the cat so tightly he growled. "You know what I meant. How can you hurt Faith like this, a woman who trusts you? And your mother? Don't you have any feelings at all?"

As if he had changed his mind and decided to pounce on her after all, he covered the space with long, agile strides. Beneath the smooth knit of his sweater the muscles of his chest rose and fell. He tossed the cat from her arms with one deft movement, and the insulted feline sought the safer vantage of a chair. One large hand fell heavily to her shoulder, one to her waist.

"How dare you?" she whispered in an attempt to hide her flaring panic. "Here in this place, this house?"

Painfully the fingers at her waist bit into the tender flesh beneath her clothes. She struck outward, meaning to knock his hand from her shoulder, but it availed nothing.

"Feelings?" His words rasped hoarsely. "Tell me about feelings. How do you know what I feel?"

"You're hurting me," she whimpered.

His lips curled beneath the moustache. His teeth gleamed whiter than ever in his disdain. For one blinking moment Victoria truly feared the violence in him.

"Why don't you watch *your* mother nearly die?" he said without thinking. "Then you tell me—"

The words were already spoken before Clifford realized, too late, their merciless cruelty. His jaw slackened with shocked revulsion at his blunder as Victoria paled. Her wide, childlike eyes spilled their glittering rivulets.

"I have." Her words were a soundless mime as his embrace hushed them when he crushed her in his arms.

"Oh, baby!" he groaned. "Oh, Victoria love."

But she only wanted to flee from the pain, the ripping jealousy and the awful self-blame. She tried to wrench herself free of his trapping arms. Tears blinded her, but she shook them off her face. Her feet struck clumsily against his.

Tearing herself free, she lunged for the door. She truly loved him, she thought in a blaze of insane grief. No man could hurt a woman so much unless she loved him.

Before she reached the open space of the door Clifford closed his hands on her arms and pulled her back so forcefully that she slumped back against his chest. In his distraught action of turning her, gathering her roughly to himself in an attempt to take the wound from her and back upon himself, Clifford buried his face in her hair.

Between the strangling sobs Victoria accused him of all the things she thought he was. He denied none of them. His parted lips swept across her forehead as she railed at him. Then they found the saltiness of her tears.

"Don't cry," he begged her and kissed her eyes and her cheeks. All the while he drew her against the angles of his body until she was almost part of his muscle and bones. His crooning had no words, only the gutteral sorrow which twisted him.

In her woman's way, Victoria realized the bonds which were spinning their silky web about them, fusing them together. Shared sorrow was stronger than shared joy. Her struggles ceased to mean anything when Clifford captured her face in his hands. Hungrily he devoured her with his eyes, raking the ravaged features as if he must understand even more.

His mouth, when it dipped to find hers, didn't hesitate. Clifford parted her lips with a crushing urgency he could never have found words to say. Her head went back, and she was filled with the paralyzing taste of him.

"Meet me," he pleaded between his ravenous kisses. His hands moved down and pressed her waist to his, his legs into hers. "Later. Tonight."

Victoria shook her head in refusal, but he fastened his lips on hers again, drinking deeply. He battered at her defenses and begged with the thrust of his tongue.

"Yes," he argued and took a quick breath. "Wait for me. I'll come. I promise."

She muttered against the prickly stubble on his jaw. "No. It's wrong. Ohh, this is wrong."

His moustache pinkened her cheeks. His breath mixed with hers until there was only one breath. "Everything is wrong, sweetheart," he mumbled against the creamy hollow below her throat, "but not this. Please, love."

"I can't."

"You can." Once again his lips traveled over her face. He moaned softly, trembling as he sought her mouth again.

Behind them, Devon gently cleared his throat.

Victoria's first thought was one of disbelief. That this was not a dream struck her when Clifford's body stiffened against hers like a skilled hunter caught unaware and freezing at the danger of a snapped twig.

Images of herself as she laughed at her own brilliantly witty remark which made her appear cosmopolitan and experienced with men clouded her vision. Then she saw herself throwing back her head in outrage, pointing her finger like Lady Macbeth and swearing vengeance on Devon for such an unforgivable intrusion. Yet her lips parted in mute horror and she knew they were traitorously pink and bruised from Clifford's demanding passion.

"In time," she said with exaggerated clarity, "I may live this down. *If* I live to be a very old woman."

"I'm really sorry," Devon apologized with a sincere droop of his shoulders. "I never know what to do when this happens. Step back and make a lot of noise and come again? Or tell a joke and pretend you didn't notice?"

Victoria's breath sighed in tattered fragments. But Clifford's tone cut with the sparkling slash of a machete. "What you do not do, Devon, is make matters more embarrassing for the lady, dammit."

Thinking she would grow hysterical if she remained in this room any longer, Victoria bent to retrieve her handbag which had dropped when Clifford's kisses had drugged her. In the moments when she stooped her face was averted, and she recognized the volatile currents flashing through the room.

The tension between the two men was not, as she would have imagined, one of temper. It was more of a concern that the other did not take a step from which there was no return except grief. Victoria received the distinct impression that Devon loved his older brother very much, that he knew much more about the relationship between Clifford and Faith than Clifford had ever told him.

Well, she decided, drawing herself upright and giving her belt a tighter yank, if Devon wanted to save Clifford from himself when Clifford didn't want to be saved, they could battle it out between them. But she didn't want to watch.

"I warned you, Cliff," Devon drawled pleasantly, smiling. "I told you that someday this would happen."

Clifford's control was truly astonishing. "This is neither the time nor the place, Devon," he said quietly. "Keep out of it."

Devon shrugged. "I'm in it already. I saw what I saw. I can't help that."

"You can help making an ass of me."

Victoria was appalled when the younger brother laughed. "You've done that already, brother of mine. You ought to tell this woman what she's caught in, Cliff. The accomplice should be aware of the crime, don't you think?"

"If you two will excuse me," Victoria squeaked in a high, shrill voice.

She was walking toward the door as she spoke. But when Clifford seated himself at the desk and moved his pen rapidly across a piece of paper, she paused. She should, she supposed, wait for the list of investors now, since she had probably ruined her reputation for it.

Looking aimless, Devon strolled about the room as Clifford hastily composed his list. He straightened a still life picture which was already straight, withdrew an LP from the stereo and studied an impressionistic sketch of "Daphnis and Chloe." Bending, he scratched the cat behind its ears.

"You're parked at the college?" he asked to make small talk.

Victoria answered stiffly, "Yes."

He nodded. "Well, as soon as Cliff's finished I'll drive you right over."

"Thank you."

"It looks as if it might start raining again."

"Yes, it does."

"You certainly don't want to get caught in a storm at night."

"No."

Clifford rose, folded the list, and ran his thumbnail over the crease as if he were stalling so Devon could take the hint and leave. Devon, however, did not oblige his brother, and Victoria guessed it wasn't for her benefit at all but for Clifford's.

When Clifford stepped forward and placed the list in her hand he rotated her by her shoulders to give them as much privacy as possible. "Meet me," he asked her again inaudibly.

With a ponderous heaviness, both of spirit and of body, Victoria detached herself. She paused in the doorway as if to memorize the way he stood, his feet parted, those knowing hands of his caught in the tops of his back pockets. Turning, she felt his eyes drill into her back. She moved forward.

"Victoria!"

Her teeth clenched as she faced the flashing amber eyes.

He started to say something, hesitated, then dropped his hands. "I'll call these people tomorrow. The next day if it's necessary. Do try to be patient."

Both of them were captured on a Shakespearean stage of tragic, star-crossed consequences, neither having the freedom to say what wanted to be said.

Victoria broke the spell first. Running out of the

room, she hurried to catch up with Devon's long strides as he opened a side door onto the long, sweeping drive. Only part of her came, as part of her stayed behind, drifting about the lonely office with Clifford and his cat, wanting to say she was sorry and not knowing how.

The parking lot at William and Mary College was deserted when Devon pulled up beside her jeep. The headlights glanced off the beaded raindrops outside to create a thousand shining prisms.

"I'll be all right, Devon," Victoria assured him and reached for the handle to her door before the car stopped rolling. She feared to linger here; the sooner she got away the less tempted she would be to wait for Clifford.

"I know you will be. You'll be fine, and so will Cliff. He's really a remarkable man, even if he is my brother."

In a way, Devon was as much of a puzzle as his daring older brother. His features were as gentle, as sensitive as Clifford's, yet without the moody thoughtfulness. From the very first moment she had liked Devon. He was uncomplicated, direct, and she was certain that he would welcome the chance to talk.

He began opening his door. "If you ever need to talk, Victoria," he said, "you can trust me."

Victoria's quizzical look seemed to offer him the invitation he was looking for. He studied her, then cocked his head. "I once told Clifford, when he decided to marry Faith, that he was throwing his life away. He didn't care, he said, and I had no choice but to accept that. Now he's caught in a bind."

She avoided asking "what bind?" Instead she said, "Some people are givers. My mother always told me

I give too much. 'Be a little selfish' she would say. Well, I still give too much, and I can understand, I think, why Clifford has arranged his life as he has."

Devon laughed. "Hell, I understand it. I don't agree with it, but I understand it. I just don't want to see someone like you get hurt. You're a sweet kid, Victoria. Stay that way."

She twisted a face at him. "I'm not a kid. And I don't wany anyone to get hurt, most of all Faith. That's assuming there's something 'going on' between Clifford and me, which there certainly is not. I mean, there never could be anything except this legal thing. In the first place . . ." She dwindled down to a broken sputter.

"You really are special, aren't you?" He chuckled and closed a friendly hand over hers. The callouses felt strange against the softness of her hand. "Special," he repeated, "and blind as a bat."

"Blind?"

"You're wrong about Faith. She wouldn't be hurt by this thing you say is not going on. I like Faith, I really do. She's honest and exactly what her name implies, but she doesn't love Clifford any more than he loves her. She loves Mother in an admirably unselfish way. But that's not enough to build a marriage on. No, you'd be the one to get hurt, Victoria. Please don't do that. Please don't get your heart broken."

Victoria watched him swing out of the car, saw him caught in relief against the hazy glow of a streetlight. She had always believed that real friendship existed from the beginning, a thing of the heart, often without words or reason. This was such a time; she knew she could trust Devon Pennington.

"Thank you," she said as she fished in her purse for her car keys. She walked with him across the wet pavement. When she climbed into the jeep, conscious of her contradiction in her petite coat and shoes, he threw back his head in laughter.

"Nice car," he said, grinning.

"It's a family tradition," she retorted. "I'm comfortable with it. Goodnight, Devon."

He tipped an imaginary hat and twirled a pretended moustache. "Ah, yes, your ladyship," he said with an affected British accent. "And if you should come upon an exceptionally dull and boring evening, do give me a call. In the book, you know. At your service."

She bowed from the waist then started the engine with a sputter. Devon closed her door and leaned near to talk to her through the vinyl window.

"If Clifford weren't my brother," he called out, "I'd say what the hell and chase you myself."

Inclining her teasing head toward his, she squinted at him. "You're not a chaser, Devon. You're the catch!"

She watched him chuckle as he walked away. Slipping the car into gear, she drove across the vacant parking spaces to the fringe of trees which guarded the campus. Her headlights dipped, and she aimed along a street of residences already shutting off the lights for the night. Without asking herself why when the answer was all too clear, she turned at the corner and drove around the block. When she returned to the parking lot Devon was gone. For a long, thoughtful moment she remembered Clifford's arms about her and the intensity in his voice when he buried his face in the curve of her throat and pleaded with her to wait for him.

"Stupid, stupid, stupid," she cursed herself. What was she doing here like some silly high school girl craving a glimpse of the football star? Was he kissing

Faith goodnight this very minute? Oh, God, was there the slightest chance that he would change his life for her? Could he possibly, *possibly* be as lonely for her as she was for him?

She hoped he was, damn him! She jammed the accelerator and screeched from the curb. She would go home, and then she would forget him.

Victoria drove, bent over the steering wheel as though the bones in her had suddenly dissolved. Ugly tears contorted her face, but who cared? Who would see? It began to rain again; quite fitting, she thought.

Not in a mood to be generous, she berated herself without a glimmer of pity. She was one of those pathetic women who persisted in getting hung up on the impossible man when a perfectly wonderful one was right in front of her nose. Why couldn't she be attracted to Devon? He was a marvelously honest man, brilliant in his own special way, an utter delight who would put her on a pedestal and never covet someone else. Why didn't that sweet pain surge through her heart when *he* smiled, instead of his beast of a brother?

Instinctively she swerved the jeep when headlights zoomed up behind her like a meteor. From the corner of her vision she recognized the unyielding lines of Clifford's Porsche when it roared up beside her, allowing her only inches in which to pull over to the curb.

She sat shivering with apprehension as he left his car parked in the middle of the street, its door open, and stepped into the glare of her headlights. Unexpected pleasure flicked along her nerves, along with dread at the thought of what he might do.

The door was jerked open beneath her hand. Clifford threw one foot up onto the rim of the frame and bent his dark wet head nearer her own.

"Where're you goin', ma'am?" he drawled like a villain out of a grade-B movie.

Unsmiling, she said: "To a quiet institution for those who do dumb things and know better. What are you doing out here in the rain?"

"Finding you, of course." His brows rippled into a frown. "You didn't wait for me."

"That surprises you? Look, Clifford, I have to get along. It's going to storm."

"You're right, it is. And you're not going any-where, sweetheart. Not on those tires."

Reaching over her, catching her completely by surprise, he flicked off the engine and daringly pock-eted her keys.

It wasn't that Clifford's boldness shocked her; nothing he could do would surprise her. But her sensitivities still smarted from the hopelessness of his mother's struggle for recovery. She needed the con-solation of knowing she still controlled some portion of her life.

"What's wrong with my tires?" she demanded much too defensively. That was a mistake, since he had been pressed about as far as a man would go.

"Only about ten thousand miles too many," he answered with more patronization than she felt ob-liged to tolerate. With an impolite disregard of her reserved aloofness he crawled in beside her. His long body didn't fit easily into her small space, and he looked so uncomfortable with his knees apart, his head nearly touching the top, that she found the entire thing absurd.

He smiled, then seemed to remember his purpose for coming. "Don't you ever look out for your own safety, Miss Carroll?"

His smoothness sent a warning flicking along her

nerves. "Are you telling me I need a man to do that for me, Mr. Pennington?"

Clifford met her glaring eyes in the gentle glow of the dash. But no humor danced in his own golden look, either. It locked with hers, and he spoke quietly, in a steady, authoritative tone he had never used with her before.

"No, Victoria. I'm simply telling you that I'm driving you home. Now don't make an unpleasant scene which will only waste time. Lock this thing up if you can and get in my car."

Her first impression of danger was in the pit of her stomach. The tension quickened and finally reached her brain. In an earnest battle of wills over this, she honestly didn't know who would be the victor. She guessed that Clifford—in his present mood—would be a very bad loser. She was certain of it when an uncompromising circle of powerful fingers closed about her wrist.

"Do it now," he said softly.

"Clifford—"

He didn't smile. "Now."

Without another word she turned the catch on the door and scooped up her purse. The jeep was parked on a quiet well-ordered street. It would be exactly as she left it when she returned, she knew.

Refusing to meet his eyes or even speak when he slid out of the cramped seat, she allowed herself to be neatly and efficiently bundled into the dry interior of the Porsche. Control was imperative now! Everything depended on remaining sensible, she thought desperately. But how could she remain sensible when every time she closed her eyes she could still see the two of them standing in the empty hallway of William and Mary College. *I feel it, too,* he had said. Could he feel it now—her fear of how this might end?

Chapter Six

It wasn't until Brayntree Estate lay five miles ahead of them that Victoria said her first word to Clifford. For nearly half an hour she had huddled in her seat. The stereo was silent; only the steady hypnotic sound of the windshield wipers and the purr of the engine broke the quiet spell. His physical presence seemed overwhelming—a power, a force that invaded everything like closing one's eyes and still being able to see the light. The years of experience he had stored away in his head would intimidate her if she let them.

She kept her gaze fixed straight ahead. "There was really nothing wrong with my tires, was there?"

Clifford tossed her a swift glance. "You want the truth?"

"Nooo," she drew out the word. "Tell me some more lies, Pennington."

He grimaced at her sarcasm. "Well," he drawled, "actually your tires would have made it. But in a downpour like this one I didn't want you out at night alone."

She chose not to respond to his implied concern.

"It's taken me thirty-two years to find you," he added softly, "and I don't want anything to happen to you now."

Frustrated, she began rolling the strip of the seatbelt into a tight, frenzied cylinder. "I wish you wouldn't say things like that."

"Why, hasn't any man ever told you the truth before?"

She flung the woven strap of nylon to the floor and dropped her cheek to the cool dampness of the window.

"I don't need a man to tell me the truth, Pennington. I know the truth when I hear it."

"You mean, you don't want *me* telling you the truth."

"I didn't say that!"

Clifford swept the car off the highway. The road through Brayntree's gates twisted. Gradually the car slowed to a crawl. "I'll make a bargain with you then, darling."

She smiled sadly without looking in his direction. "I don't trust a bargain with you. Somehow I think I would wind up the loser. I'm sure of it."

His chuckle was mirthless. "It doesn't seem to me that either of us is on any great winning streak right now. What have you got to lose?"

The gravel crunched beneath the wide tires as they came to a decided stop. Victoria lifted a slender finger of warning.

"For one thing, I've got this to lose." She threw out her hand toward the great building which neither of them could clearly distinguish in the storm, except for several blurred yellow rectangles of lighted windows. "I learned a long time ago a person couldn't have everything. You aren't the first man who's ever kissed me, Pennington. That man wanted to make bargains, too. Him for Brayntree."

He flicked off the engine. "I'm not asking you to give up Brayntree. Why the hell do you think I'm trying to satisfy both clients of this case if I want you to give up Brayntree? I know what it means to you."

She sniffed her disbelief. "You couldn't possibly. It's all I've ever wanted."

Victoria was certain he said the word 'idiot' under his breath, and her temper flashed like the ragged streak of lightning which darted across the liquid sky.

"Why are we talking about Brayntree, Clifford? We both know what the real thorn is here. You've obligated your life to a perfectly decent woman, and you've let your eyes wander from the straight and narrow."

"Oh hell, Victoria!" He swiveled on the seat, and his knee jammed sharply against her leg. She stared at the strong flex of it. "You've got a tongue like a whip. Have I once lied to you?"

Her voice was toneless. "You've conveniently forgotten to tell me things."

Clifford's middle three fingers angrily scoured over his moustache. Then his hand cut a brisk path through the space which separated them, slicing the anger. "Okay, okay. From this point forward there'll be no more games between us, no more hedging, no more pussyfooting around the truth. Agreed?"

"That's another thing, Pennington. You keep assuming something is between us, and I keep telling you—"

"No lies, I said!"

His fingers clamped over her mouth as he drew her head back against the seat. When she took a quick breath against his hand he dropped it and touched the center of his forehead.

"No lies, Victoria. No pride. At least, between ourselves let's tell it like it is. You know damn well something is between us."

She shook her head violently, sending her hair tumbling. "You move too fast for me, Clifford," she whispered as she twisted a button on her coat. It fell off in her hand and she frowned at it. Absently she stuffed it in her pocket.

His knee continued to press into her thigh. "If Faith weren't in my life, would you talk about it?" he urged her.

Victoria's head dropped even lower, and she grasped a lock of hair and pulled it, twisting it mercilessly. "But she is in your life. It's not as simple as knowing there is another woman, as they say. She's woven into your family, Clifford, with your mother and a lot of other things I can't cope with."

She realized, when Clifford straightened his shoulders and let out his breath in disappointment, that he wouldn't force her to talk about it anymore.

"Come on," he said wearily, "I'll walk you to the door."

Hot tears pressed painfully behind her eyes. "In this downpour?"

"Naturally. I won't mildew."

"Around the west side then," she answered. "To my rooms." ·

She flipped up the collar to her coat. Was this the end of it, then? Well, she had come close to touching it, whatever it had been—love, fulfillment, delusion.

As if he read her thoughts Clifford spoke through

the darkness. "You know we'll never feel quite this way again, don't you? Not ever again."

Her breath made a long harsh sound. "Are you—"

"Victoria, I want to kiss you."

Her next breath was more difficult as she struggled not to cry. "Are you ready to make a run for it?"

Clifford sighed to himself. "I'm ready when you are."

"We're making a habit of getting soaked together!" Victoria gasped a moment later as she fumbled with her key, her fingers half-frozen.

Close on her heels, Clifford towered over her, his arms encasing her as he bent near to protect her from the drive of the rain with his back. Victoria wasn't certain if her chattering teeth were from the chill of the rain or the feel of his legs molded powerfully to the backs of hers.

Darkness, thick and soupy, isolated the west wing entrance to Brayntree. Her apartment had been selected with care, far enough from the main upstairs dormitory to prevent her from being such an integral part of it. Occasionally she had complained about the inconvenience of it. But now, coming in with a man in the middle of the night, she was thankful she wouldn't be the object of prying, girlish eyes.

"If I continue running around with you, girl," Clifford declared between clenched teeth, "I might mildew after all. Give me that key."

His left hand already encircled her waist. Reaching about her with his right, he lifted the key from her trembling fingers. Victoria shivered as he inserted it into the seemingly invisible lock. When he turned the key and pushed open the door, she practically tumbled from his arms into the welcome haven of the hallway.

"This has all the makings of good slapstick," he

joked lightly as Victoria groped over the wall for the light switch.

Immediately the hall glowed from twinkling sconces mounted on the heavily-grained panels of walnut. Clifford glanced around himself, taking in the one part of the estate he had not ventured into when he and Ed Barnes had made their fateful visit. At his feet a pool of water spread.

From a safe distance she gazed at him. His jeans clung immodestly to his legs, dripping, and his hair was plastered to his head in shadowy ringlets. Glistening rivulets trailed down the muscles of his neck and disappeared into the collar of his jacket. Droplets trembled from the fragile ledge of his moustache, glittered, then fell.

"You're wet," she said ludicrously.

He reached to pluck a clinging lock from her own forehead, but she pulled away, fearful of his familiarities.

His hand dropped to his side. "Is that a fact?"

In the distance thunder rolled across the heavens in muffled growling sentences, as if offering a troubled observation of their circumstances. Half expecting someone to appear through one of the adjoining doors and gasp at them, Victoria searched about herself, then back at him.

"Well!" she said briskly and rubbed her hands together. "Here we are."

His brows lifted. "Yes, here we are."

"I suppose," she said as she waved her fingers at his soaked condition, "you could use a towel before you go back home."

"That would be nice."

Despite her mounting irritation at bearing another of his inspections, Clifford let his gaze ramble over her bedraggled state. Her dishabille, her uninitiated nervousness aroused him more than any display of erotic fancy ever could. He tingled with a warm low ache, the need to protect her. At the same time he wanted to explain how frightened he was of losing her. She wasn't the kind of woman who would settle for an open-ended relationship, and he didn't know, at this moment, how to free himself for her. Only that he *must*. And it must be done delicately, for she must never be burdened with guilt for breaking up a love affair that didn't even exist.

The magnitude of the pain he could inflict upon innocent people staggered him. He shifted his weight and watched her eyes snap to attention.

Knowing a moment of dismay for ever inviting him in, Victoria realized her thoughts had drifted. "Towels!" she gasped. "Ahh, I'll get some. Wait here."

Danger was breathing down the back of his neck, Clifford thought. "I'll be here," he promised.

Victoria disappeared from the room to slump against the wall outside the door, fighting to catch her breath. How could she turn all liquid when he admired her with his eyes? Why hadn't she had the courage to simply ask him to go? To stay away from her? It would take her months, years to get over this, if she ever could. She didn't care how much he loved his mother, or how meaningless his engagement was. She couldn't handle it.

Around a corner she positioned herself before the floor-to-ceiling linen closet that served the entire school. She wrenched open its door, then stood staring at it before she could remember what she had come here to do.

Being quite careful not to meet Clifford's eyes when she returned, Victoria thrust several towels at his chest. Then, thinking they would look much less suspicious in her room than standing out in the hall, she threw open the door to her suite and stepped inside.

Even with the high ceiling, the huge room managed to achieve the effect of warmth and coziness, due primarily to a wise selection of pink wallpaper and femininely-patterned draperies. One antique lamp was lit on a small table beside the four-poster bed, and its glow cast gentle, suggestive shadows across the richly waxed floor. The plush rug which spread before the fireplace soaked the shadows into its rose depths. A woman's room—soothing and uncluttered.

Clifford smiled his appreciation for her impeccable taste. "This suits you," he said simply without expecting a reply.

The deep huskiness of his voice alarmed her even more, and she hurriedly unbuttoned her coat, dropping it into a neat fold beside the door. She stepped out of her soggy shoes and left them beside it. Crossing the rug in damp pantyhose, she attempted to revive the warm coals in the fireplace. They stubbornly refused to catch, and she replaced the poker with a troubled sigh.

Turning, she flinched at the thoroughly masculine sight of Clifford bending forward, blotting his hair, then removing his jacket with smooth, fluid motions. It was such a thoughtless thing for him to do, she felt, to place a lasting memory of himself into this room. He stood holding the crumpled towel. Not knowing what else to do, she stepped quickly and removed it from his hands.

"Well, I'll be going now," he said presently. "Thank you for the towel."

She nodded. "You're welcome. And . . . thank you for driving me home."

His large hand loosely circled the doorknob.

"And for the list, of course," she added lamely. "I forgot that."

It was as if the sound of her voice placed a detaining hand on his arm. He glanced about the room, and considered the fire for a moment as it drizzled its dismal threads of smoke up the chimney. "Would you like me to build you a fire before I go?"

"I—"

Before she could refuse he stepped to the hearth and stooped. His back was bent, and she imagined it bronzed and naked beneath the palms of her hands. She imagined him lowering himself on her, his weight crushing her.

Hurriedly she moved to a closet and pulled out a floor-length velvet wraparound skirt and a cranberry-hued blouse. They didn't exactly match, and her underthings lay folded in a bureau some feet past him. But stepping that near him was foolhardy. She clutched them tightly and disappeared.

Ten minutes later when she emerged from the bathroom a small fire blazed brightly, cheering the whole room. Clifford was wringing out his socks and smoothing them to dry before the flames. Both their coats were hung on a rack beside the door, and his shoes rested intimately beside her petite ones. Even her footprints across the rug had been tidily mopped up.

She eyed his bare feet and attempted to steady herself by the sheer strength of her will. "You certainly do have a way of making yourself at home, Pennington," she observed, her words sounding brittle and high.

He smiled and let his eyes touch the gleam of the firelight in her hair. Energy virtually sparkled across the room when his gaze fell lower, lingering at the sultry outline of her breasts as they moved beneath the clinging blouse. Without thinking, she glanced downward. She flushed as she watched her nipples tighten with expectancy.

Clifford's tongue flicked across his upper lip, and one hand lifted to nervously smooth back his hair. Unable to control the impulse to shield herself, Victoria fluttered her fingers to her throat. His grin was shattering.

"There's a comb on the vanity," she choked.

Without a word Clifford stepped to her burled walnut dressing table. But even as he bent his knees to drop himself down within view of the mirror, he searched for her in the reflection. Feeling as if she were a stupid, hapless moth repeatedly darting into the flame, she met his eyes. He outlasted her, and she whirled away with a small murmur of panic.

"I'm embarrassing you," he said as he tossed the comb aside. "I apologize. I forget you're still a—"

"Don't say I'm a girl!" she blurted, still not facing him. "And it's perfectly all right for you to dry your things here." Her voice dwindled dejectedly. "There's nothing wrong in that."

She sensed him moving about the room, and she flicked at her fingernails, then chewed at one.

"We're pretty predictable, after all," he said.

"What do you mean?"

"Oh, behaving like a couple of kids fencing, so tongue-tied we can't talk about anything except the weather without going to pieces."

She shrugged. "It's a kind of protection, I think. For me, at least."

"Do you think you need protection from me?"

She spun to face him. "Yes!" she cried before she realized what an incriminating admission it was, like confessing that he opened her up, exposed her.

The fire popped loudly, sending a shower of bril-

liant sparks sailing up the chimney. She started, and
Clifford pursed his mouth as if he had made an
important point. With a discouraged sigh he tested
his socks for dryness, dropped to the hearth and
began pulling them on. She didn't move but grew
entranced with the neat sensuality of his legs in the
tight jeans. Snapping up his head, he caught her in
the act of watching. But he didn't embarrass her this
time; he took his jacket from the hook beside the
door and wriggled into it.

"I might—" she blurted.

"What?"

Victoria smoothed the waist of her skirt and wiped
her damp hands down the sides. "I could," her palm
turned upward in her unfamiliar step as aggressor, "I
mean, I might get you something to eat before you
drive back. You didn't have any dinner. Or anything.
That is . . . if you want me to. I don't want to keep
you if—" Things were going miserably, she thought.
Her breath sounded as if she had been running for
hours.

Clifford's smile was dazzling. "That's the best thing
you've said all evening."

A bank robber couldn't possibly have felt more
furtive than she did as she leaned back against a wall
in the corridor, pressing the back of her hand to her
lips. If one of her students were to walk downstairs
and see her like this she would be absolutely shattered.

Her hands were still shaking as she laid out a large
tray and smoothed a crisp napkin over the bottom.
She placed two extra napkins upon it, then two
long-stemmed glasses, found a bottle of aged burgun-
dy and a chunk of German cheese. After slicing
several pieces of Mamie's bread and putting them on
a china plate, she washed two pears. She was, on

sheer romantic impulse, arranging two chrysanthemums in one of Helen's crystal decanters when
Stephanie's voice made her drop it to the stainless
countertop with a thunk.

"I couldn't imagine who in the world would be
fussing around in the kitchen in the middle of the—"

The other woman, clad in her bathrobe, her hair
streaming down the center of her back, approached
as she spoke. She paused for an awkward moment,
saw the tray set for two and allowed her gaze to
interpret Victoria's alluring skirt and blouse.

"Oh, dear," she whispered as Victoria retrieved
the vase and the flowers and placed them emphatically on the tray. "Oh dear, oh dear."

"He drove me home in the storm, Stephanie," she
said in a decidedly level tone. "Don't go getting
strung out about it. Neither of us has eaten since
noon. That's all there is to it."

"I see," Stephanie replied, obviously not believing
any of it.

Stephanie drew herself a glass of water and opened
one of the tall cabinet doors. She pushed a chair to
the countertop and climbed onto it as Victoria
gawked in amazement. After fishing behind some
canisters for a moment, she produced a half-empty
package of cigarettes.

Sighing, Victoria picked up the tray. "Do I do that
to you? Drive you to a prolific case of lung conges-
tion?"

"No," Stephanie whispered. She lit the cigarette
from the pilot light on the large oven which monopolized one end of the kitchen. "But you don't help
any. Am I supposed to give you some sage warning
about not getting yourself hurt?"

Flipping off the light, leaving only the glimmer of
an all-night light in a corner pantry, Victoria began

walking out the door. "You're not supposed to do anything. My eyes aren't sealed shut."

Behind her Stephanie coughed. "Somehow I don't feel better."

"Your friend knew Clifford a long time ago. He's different now."

"People don't change that much."

The deserted hallway was tense and threatening on this night, Victoria thought. Of all people she would rather have kept in ignorance about Clifford's presence at Brayntree it was this woman, her dearest friend.

"Maybe not," Victoria said in a dismissing manner. "And maybe they do. Maybe things aren't what they seem."

They walked the distance to Stephanie's room without speaking again. Outside the door, which was separated from Victoria's room by the entire length of the wing, Stephanie touched the younger woman's cheeks with halting fingertips. It was a familiarity she seldom took.

"Be careful. No one but a fool goes swimming where there are known sharks."

Victoria laughed, tossing her head. "You never were a very good swimmer, silly."

The fatigue about Stephanie's eyes produced a conglomeration of emotions in Victoria: irritation, affection, understanding, appreciation. She wanted to say, *Don't worry about me, I'm over twenty-one.* But that wouldn't help, so they murmured goodnight in a slightly withdrawn mood, and Victoria paused outside her own door. Later, much later, she would think about what Stephanie had said. But now, at this moment, she only wanted to sit with Clifford for a few quiet moments and look at him without being interrupted. What was so risky in that? She only wanted to dangle her toes in the surf, not swim out over her head!

The firelight sent capricious images dancing about the room as she and Clifford sat cross-legged before the hearth. As the gold and amber flames gradually warmed her cheeks and tantalized her chilled limbs, the richness of the wine flowed through her veins. Her senses began to tingle with a feeling of pleasant well-being, and her guilt of the afternoon finally retreated to a more quiet, less bothersome part of her mind.

Still, she remained oddly silent as she carved the cheese into small thin slivers and placed the knife back on a napkin. Just knowing that Clifford stretched languorously on his side near her, propped on his elbow, was as heady as the wine.

"There!" she said and lifted a fragile goblet from the tray. She inched to a chair sitting behind her and pulled her knees close. She arranged her long skirt in a modest way and prudently refrained from looking directly at him.

Clifford bit into his pear with a crisp crunch. "What did you and Devon talk about in the car?" he asked lightly.

The question astonished her. "Nothing," she hedged, sipping more than she intended.

"I doubt that, knowing Devon as I do."

Pretending to be absorbed with her wine, she swirled it languidly in her glass. Her voice was husky when she replied. "What do you think we talked about?"

Clifford sat up straight, then rose to amble about her room. Occasionally he sipped from his glass as he studied her collection of private womanly things. He removed the stopper from a bottle of perfume and moved it slowly beneath his nose as if he savored it.

Then he sent her a satisfied grin. From perusing her bookcase he strolled to her stereo.

"Ah," he said, placing his glass on a table. "Rachmaninoff's E Minor."

She smiled but said nothing.

He slipped the shining disk of vinyl from the plastic shield and held it toward the light of the fire. "They say this is the most romantic melody ever written," he mused.

"You surprise me, Clifford. I would never have guessed you were a lover of good music."

He laughed. "Willie Nelson is more my style, hmm?"

He was touching too deeply, she thought. He was spilling into the empty spaces of her life, was fitting into lonely corners of her room as if he belonged there. She felt her head ring with sirens of warning.

"I like Willie Nelson," she added.

"So do I." He sent her an odd look. "Which movement is the celebrated one, love?"

Victoria, knowing he must leave while some of her strengths were still intact, began replacing items on the tray. "The first," she answered without looking.

"Liar," he laughed deep in his chest, mocking her. "It's the Adagio, and you know it."

As he lowered the needle to the spinning disc, one of the loveliest melodies ever penned filled the room. Tantalizing and sweet, it slowly paralyzed her with the sensuality of its spell; it pulsed with the throb of her own responding heartbeat.

Victoria stopped breathing when he folded his long body at her feet and leaned his elbows on his knees. She looked dumbly at her own bare toes peeping from beneath her skirt.

Like a child reciting "this little piggy went to market," Clifford idly touched a fingertip to one toe, then another. "I suspect you and Devon talked about my . . . engagement. About how stupid I am, how I've been throwing my life away."

He slipped back into the conversation so easily—not looking into her eyes, caressing each toe as some men would smooth a coin—that Victoria couldn't have been less prepared for the impact. When he lifted one of her feet in his hands and dipped his head to press his lips to the curve of her arch, a shiver ran through her. It was so yearning, so draining. She flailed behind her for the security of the chair. The kisses he strewed up her ankle were gossamer, featherlight from parted lips. He cupped her calf in his palm.

"I don't think we should talk about you and Faith. It won't solve anything," she choked, which was foolish since Faith was already forgotten.

"Why not?"

The tip of his tongue began tracing gauzy patterns over the knee cradled in his hands.

Victoria stirred to prevent him from continuing and the folds of her skirt fell away, shimmering with careless grace into pools of wine-dark velvet. Before she could gather them up both their eyes fixed on the invitation of her pale, gleaming thigh. All the strengths Victoria had ever supposed herself to possess dissolved when she stared at the whiteness of her own fair skin.

"Because it's none of my business!" she cried and distraughtly flung herself upward, fearing the deadly seduction of his hands now.

Immediately he was behind her. His hands fanned her waist with ease, and his legs encroached into the deep swirls of velvet. "Victoria?"

"I think you should go," she whispered.

Clifford's desire was fiery—indurate and unden-iable—as it pressed into the folds of her skirt. As he drew her back against his chest, one hand closed possessively over the swell of her breast and the other shaped the subtle, feminine bones below her waist. The curve of her neck beckoned to him like a charm, and she whimpered when he buried his face into it.

"I don't love her," he muttered thickly and took the lobe of her ear in his teeth.

Threatened, sensing her peril, the virgin in Victoria sent her spinning from his embrace. "What kind of a man are you?" she gasped, slightly bent, trying to breathe. "This is wrong!"

In blind agony she knelt beside the tray and attempted to gather the items which only moments before had brought them pleasure. She wasn't certain, even as it happened to her, if she wanted him to ignore her hollow protests or not. But he was beside her, prying the clattering glass from her hands, saying something she didn't understand. Tears scalded her eyes, and she pressed them back with the heels of her hands. Stumbling, she managed to get to her feet.

His arms went about her knees tighter than he meant for them to, and she lost her precarious balance. Collapsing against the rock of his shoulders, she flung her arms about his head to keep from falling. As if he were a wandering youth whose steps had wearied of tracing and retracing the same monotonous path, he crushed his face into her skirt. Gently he rocked her in his arms, back and forth, repeating her name.

"It's all right," she comforted, stroking the dark locks of his hair, not even certain of what she meant. "It's all right."

But as she cradled his head, she stilled. Gradually she became conscious of the wandering play of Clifford's fingers. His hands loosened their clasp of her knees and slid silkily upward. With surprising skill he manipulated the flap of her skirt and smoothed the naked length of her thigh. As his fingers closed into that curve, that baby-soft swell which had tempted his eyes so often, she drew in her breath sharply.

"Clifford!" Her protest came without meaning when a surge of relentless heat blistered her own body. She knew the wild sensation of drowning in fire. "You . . . ought to . . . go."

"I know," he groaned.

His breath was searing her skin through the traitorous velvet. Somewhere, as he caressed the backs of her legs with widespread hands, a clock struck one shimmering beat.

"It's late," she breathed, drugged now but still fighting his invasion.

"In a minute." His words came muffled, ragged. "Just a minute."

But even as he talked, his fingers were growing impatient, confronting the resistance of her knees. Victoria struggled intuitively—a frightened doe shrinking from the path of the predator. Her attempts to retrieve his hands were frantic and futile when he ventured boldly, with a determination as old as man. He searched out the moist, sensual secrets known only to her, and she thought she was lost.

His discovery was driving, relentless. Her eyes, glazed with desire, saw nothing and her ears hardly heard his grated murmurs of pleasure. "You want me," he told her hoarsely.

"Yes." Now her hands, which had persisted in

their hindrance, acted of their own accord. She twisted against him, surrendering, taking short, deep breaths.

"Help me," he choked, and she pressed his hands in a knowing way, teaching him, thrilling him. She held her last crystalline breath until the bubble sparkled and burst over her head to cascade and slowly disappear into a shadowy calm.

It was, in the end, a matter of trust. With every vow of love Clifford uttered—not eloquently now but brokenly—their transgression dwindled in enormity. Breathing hard, he scooped her up and cradled her to his chest, his lips parted and unsmiling. His head bent and he crushed her mouth with the fierce hunger of a man who has waited too many years. She accepted the urgency of his tongue, not because he wanted her so badly, but because he needed her so much that his graceful hands trembled when he lowered her to the big bed.

His pleasure when he saw her the first time amazed her. He looked at the flawless curves, her pale, straining breasts, her sleek firmness. In the shadows of the firelight he leaned back on his heels and briefly closed his eyes with a sigh. His hands rested shakily upon his knees.

"I knew you would be this beautiful," he said. His shoulders drooped as if he had come to the end of a tiring journey. "I imagined you exactly this way."

One fingertip ventured to trace the side of her breast, over the incredibly pink crest to tease it awake. His breath caught. "Oh God, Victoria!" he confessed gravely. "I feel as new as you do, like nothing that has ever happened to me before."

Victoria felt as if nothing was settled between them because their future led nowhere. In a last desperate need to explain why she must not, *could not* do this thing, she threaded her fingers through his. "Oh, Clifford, I can't. Please understand. Please try."

"It's okay," he said, meaning it. "It's okay. We can wait."

Deep in the secret corners of his mind he truly meant to wait. He was the grown man, the responsible one. She was the innocent. He must be the pillar, the strength.

"I'll go now," he promised and groped for the honeyed dew of her mouth one last time.

It was a promise whispered into the caprice of the wind. Yielding, for her, was as destined as the inevitable power of his knee which buried itself deeper and deeper between her own. It was as certain as the aroused male force which swiftly overpowered him. They both knew, then, that he wouldn't leave her, that they wouldn't wait. The boundary had been crossed.

"Be gentle with me!" she begged him.

But she knew, even as her back arched with the sterling grace of a bow, even as her tiny cry marked something she would never give again, that he could be no other way than gentle. He gathered her to himself with grave self-control. Then, reaching for her soul, he poured himself into her in the first completely selfless act of his life.

Only in the spent shadows of passion and the quiet return to reality did Victoria suffer the consequence of being Helen Carroll's daughter. She regretted, not their love which was beyond doubt, but that they had not been strong enough to first be certain of where they stood. So she lay quietly and pressed her cheek against the hard, elastic muscles of his waist. His breaths came more steadily now, yet she knew he didn't sleep.

Clifford roused at the wetness of her tears on him. His head lifted, and he stirred to draw her up into his arms. "Oh, love," he whispered into her hair, smoothing it, "don't cry. Please don't cry."

"I'm sorry. I don't mean to. It's just that . . ."

"That, what?" he crooned.

He had been perfect, loving her so totally. How could she say the words? "Nothing," she sighed and blotted her cheeks.

The sense of loss Clifford suffered was a bereavement of something once dreamed and misplaced. He admitted to himself as he stared at the masonry marks above his head on the ceiling, that he didn't know Victoria nearly as well as he should. His instincts were good, and he knew the delicate care he had taken was more than worth it. Yet her own fulfillment was still a mystery. It could not account for the sadness she bore now. What had he done that was so terribly bad? Hadn't he promised her he would place the affairs of his life in order for her? What had she needed, marriage first?

"Victoria?"

Before she answered, the silver echo of three chimes sounded in the distance. "What?"

"Talk to me."

"What do you want me to say?"

"What you feel."

For a while she didn't reply. Then she slipped from the haven of his arms and, turning on her side, drew her knees up tightly beneath her chin. From her blanketed huddle she whispered, "I don't want to need you."

Frowning, thinking she would turn back to him, Clifford closed his hand over her shoulder. "It's not a failure to need someone, sweetheart. Needing makes the world go 'round."

"I can't need you. And we can't ever do this again."

Clifford could understand her independent pride—she had been trained by an obvious master, Helen Carroll. But he couldn't accept her refusal to make love with him.

"Darling, I know it's important to you, having things all wrapped up. I don't intend to put you through an emotional endurance test."

"You're not a free man," she protested, almost in tears.

Clifford laughed softly, then sobered at the sight of her slender, unrelenting back. "You sound like I'd have to divorce her."

"You almost do. My mother would die if she knew what I'd done. If I were Faith, I'd kill me."

"Damn it, Victoria, you haven't done anything! Except something quite wonderful. Will you be sensible?"

Blinking away the glassy blurring, she rolled over and searched for the resentment she was certain was on his face. What she saw was more like despondency. "I know what I can't do, Clifford."

"Darling—"

"Men look at things like this differently than women," she grieved, her remorse very real and just as hopeless to reason with.

"Oh, hell," he muttered. He tightened his arms around her waist and attempted to draw her against the length of his body. Stiffening, Victoria refused to allow it. He absently brushed wisps of her hair back from her eyes and arranged them behind her ear.

"I'm not your father, Victoria, and I'm not going to run out on you. I know you have a fear of that, but believe me when I tell you that my intentions are . . . what do they say? Honorable?"

Her words were muffled in the vicinity of his chest. "So honorable you have to keep up pretenses of loving someone else?"

He sighed with weariness at the great complexity of human emotions. "Things take a little time, sweetheart. That's all I'm asking of you, time to work this out. People's feelings must be handled carefully. I can't just charge in with a hatchet and start severing ties."

She wanted to lash out, *If you really loved me you'd break everything with Faith this very minute! You'd care more about what I need than how she feels!* But she only struggled to keep her face from twisting into an ugly sob. "We have to wait, then," she said, "until things are right."

He thought he would have been able to accept her terms if she had only admitted that she needed his love. Not understanding his dismal sense of failure, he whispered that he loved her and promised everything would be all right. She nodded wordlessly and, after dressing himself, he kissed her one last time. He stepped outside into a night that looked like something out of Edgar Allan Poe. He cursed himself for not comprehending the protected virgin mind. He thought, when he pulled the car door shut behind himself, that now he knew something of the madness of poets. How was a man to know what was right when he was driven with his first real love? How was he to keep from hurting the one thing which he treasured above his own life?

He was certain he didn't have the answers. But he knew he would find them. He had to. Losing Victoria Carroll after having lived this long without her was not something he intended to let happen.

Chapter Seven

*A*fter having slept the wretched total of one hour, Victoria dragged herself to the windows and tugged open the drapes. Only the weather had any reality, cloudy and uncompromising. Bare trees shivered in the mist, and bronze chrysanthemums huddled together to keep warm. Her head, heavy with the realization of a turning point in her life, threatened to split.

Showering and getting dressed failed to dispell the eerie sensation of sleepwalking. She brushed her hair and considered her virginity, that woman's thing which carried a declining value with society as the years passed. Even to her it was an occasional embarrassment when friends lifted their brows and said with unintentional condescension, "You mean you're *still* a virge?"

So now she wasn't a "virge." And even if Clifford

was the man she wanted to change her life, she despised the sense of condemnation which came with it. She wanted to feel a sense of the future, of permanency, of belonging to his family, of sharing everything. She felt none of those things.

She was a different woman now. She looked at things differently. As surely as if he had carved his initials in her flesh, Clifford branded her, ruining her for anyone else. Until the day came when he was free to say "Marry me," she would mark time, her hands outstretched, fighting to keep his promises from passing through her fingers.

She needed time. She placed a message on her office answering device saying she was unable to come to the telephone. It was cowardly, yes, since Clifford would undoubtedly phone. But she would just barely get through her cheerful pretenses for Stephanie at mealtimes and for the girls in the classroom. Clifford's voice would undo her. And his eyes, peering into hers as he asked her to love him, would be irresistible.

That night she hardly slept at all. And the next night was, to her disappointment, little different with its vicious tormenting insomnia. And the next night. And the next . . .

Her classes suffered very little from her affair of the heart. Her skill was intuitive by now, and her only major task was camouflaging her physical despondency. Stephanie, however, was another matter entirely. Her sharp eye missed very little, and her guesses were much too accurate.

Inventing an excuse on Friday afternoon to avoid her, Victoria dressed in faded jeans and an old car coat. She left word with Mamie that she would be in the stable, tending to a long-procrastinated task. She hoped her assistant would think she had driven into Williamsburg and would wade through the accumulated office chores by herself.

The late November air blew wonderfully cold and direct. Shivering did something for a person, Victoria thought as she trudged the distance to the ivy-covered building which had fallen into dismal disrepair during the last years of Helen's life. Being cold narrowed things down to the basics of life—the need for shelter and warmth. One could hardly sit around feeling jealous over a love affair when one feared freezing to death.

"Need any help, missy?" Bud Whitaker's cracked old voice jarred Victoria from her musings of self-preservation.

"Oh!" Victoria felt the tiny scald of anger at being jerked out of her dreamworld. Spinning about to face the tall thin man swallowed by a pair of striped coveralls, a grease rag flapping reassuringly from one hip pocket, she forced herself to be pleasant. "Where did you come from, Bud? Out of the woodwork?"

He laughed his high-pitched cackle. "Not this old Johnny Reb, ma'am. I've been cussin' at that old tractor parked in the barn. Gotta have that case bored. Can't put it off another season. Otherwise, you're gonna really have a repair bill."

Victoria ran her fingers through her hair. As unreasonable as it was she was irritated at Clifford for not being available for a decision such as this. Then she felt foolish.

"You don't think we could get by with a set of rings, maybe?" she suggested. "I hate to fix the old thing just yet. I mean, if I have to put this place up for sale it'll be money thrown away, Bud."

"The old buzzard uses more oil than gas now," Bud reminded her with a doleful shake of his head. "You'd better plan to call Seth Bascomb for a complete overhaul." He squinted at her, disapproval twisting his mouth. "You can't sell this place, missy. Why, that old tractor and me've been around here since before you was born. What'd we do? Where'd we go?"

There were times when these responsibilities nearly crushed her, she thought. Putting a slender hand on his sleeve, she smiled. "Now don't you worry about that, Bud. I won't turn you out in the cold, no matter what happens. Mother couldn't have made it without you and Mamie. I haven't forgotten."

The old man appeared satisfied with her answer, and a guilty spear plunged into her as he moved away muttering about the old John Deere. How would she take care of all of them: Bud, Mamie, Brian Levy, Jack, Stephanie? How she envied women who had no more to do than worry about their personal problems. She felt like an avalanche hovered over her. One mistake and it would all go.

Heaving a weary, frightened sigh, Victoria shoved open the right door of the once well-tended stable. She hooked it securely and grabbed for the other door.

Only three horses remained at Brayntree. Once there had been a dozen. Helen had been an excellent horsewoman. She remembered sitting in front of her in the saddle, perched against her comforting back. Horseback riding was part of the curriculum at the school at one time. Each year some of the girls entered the state competitions. But now inflation had gobbled up that facility as it had a number of the others.

She paused in front of Daisy's stall. "That's all you're good for," she criticized the gentle-eyed mare whose silky nose was marked with a long-tipped star, "eating. You're eating me out of house and home, Daisy. What am I going to do with you?"

"I suggest you decide what you're going to do with yourself before you go straightening out someone else," Stephanie offered cheerfully.

Thinking that escaping her friend had been too good to be true, Victoria pasted a smile on her face and turned. Stephanie leaned against the heavy frame of the door, bundled in a hooded jacket, lined boots and a plaid muffler wrapped beneath her chin.

"Why, Steph," she chuckled, "I thought that was your job, keeping me all straightened out."

"Me? And whose else, dear, the army? You're a national threat."

Still smiling, glancing down to brush at the leg of her jeans, Victoria shrugged so slightly it was almost nonexistent. "I'm guilty on that score."

"And on the score of Clifford Pennington?" came the other woman's serious query.

It was a physical effort to refrain from rushing at Stephanie and yelling that she had no right to pry into this. Yet Victoria only smiled and touched the slight curve above her upper lip in a noncommital gesture.

"I've been catching up on some of the backed up office work, Victoria. That man has left a number of very interesting messages on the answering service."

"I don't want to hear them."

Victoria moved past Daisy's stall into the cluttered tack room. All that remained were a couple of old saddles which had seen much better days and some neglected bridles dangling on one wall. Stacked in the corner were a number of bales of hay, three empty oil drums and a tall stack of empty crates. "Ignore the messages," she called over the shoulder.

"How do you ignore someone who says he'll break your boss's face and have her arrested if she doesn't return his calls?" Stephanie's words grew more distinct as she followed Victoria into the tack room.

In spite of the seriousness of the circumstances and Clifford's very real irritation, Victoria smiled into her collar. "Clifford tends to become over-dramatic. I think it comes with the law degree."

The crunch of Stephanie's boots sounded behind her, then moved past the place where Victoria stood kicking at tufts of dirty hay. The older teacher climbed on the stack of crates which placed her several feet above the head mistress of Brayntree. She bent over her. "Did I ever tell you I once had a love affair?" she said casually.

For a moment Victoria was so surprised she could hardly put her thoughts into a sane order. She had expected Stephanie to try and give her advice, to pry out bits and pieces of what she and Clifford had done that night. She looked at her sharply, then away, beginning to pluck bits of hay from one of the bales.

"You know you haven't," she answered.

"It was terrible. I won't burden you with the details."

Victoria never ceased marveling at Stephanie's resilience. "You obviously survived it. I can't figure out why you're even telling me. Unless, of course, you figure that Clifford Pennington and I . . ." She hesitated. "Oh yes, you put two and two together and got, what? Six?"

Stephanie leaned back against the wall behind her and fished in her pocket for a cigarette. The match flared for a second, then waved back and forth until it went out. "I got the impression that someone I care for a great deal has just made a very human miscalculation."

Frowning at the ashes which Stephanie flicked down on her sneakers, Victoria kept her voice under strict control. "A miscalculation to you, perhaps."

"Do you think it's easy, watching you grieve over that two-timer?"

Spinning, presenting her friend with a view of her back, Victoria gritted her teeth. Victoria could have called Clifford a much worse name, but to hear someone else do it sent defensive fervor slamming through her veins. "He's not a two-timer, Stephanie. He's a sensitive, compassionate man. You're letting past prejudices color your judgment, based on hearsay, I might remind you."

Stephanie didn't answer immediately. "Maybe," she said, "but he nearly broke Darlene's heart back then. And he's dragging you down."

A surprising calm permeated Victoria's whole outlook. "He loves me, Steph. Don't be mistaken about that. Whatever he may have done in the past, or even in the present, he loves me."

"He told you that?"

"Yes."

At least Stephanie didn't accuse her of naiveté. It wasn't often that Victoria was this firm with her, but when she was, even if Stephanie disagreed to the point of bursting, she held her opinions in restraint.

"Besides," Victoria felt she should explain though she hated doing it, "there are circumstances. How can I blame Clifford for doing what I would probably do if I were in his place?"

She removed a bridle from the wall, and it cracked as she fingered the old leather. Without disagreeing,

Stephanie blew a lazy stream of smoke at the roof-line.

"I can see there's no convincing you otherwise," she said. "Believe me, pet, when I say I understand. And I sympathize. I wouldn't listen, either, when it happened to me. I won't ask you if you're in love with him. Those circles under your eyes tell me enough."

The only answer to that question was Daisy munching her grain. Victoria, burying her fingers into a bale of hay, limberly climbed up to sit beside her friend. With their legs crossed, they were bent over like a pair of wizened Indians having a pow-wow. Victoria absently peeled off slivers of wood from a crate and threw them outward, and watched them fall to the dirt floor.

"I really don't know what else to do but put Brayntree up for sale, Steph. I've done nothing but think about it since Clifford . . . well, since that night." She went on rather hastily. "I know it's pride, but I can't let him help me with this. I'm too involved with him already, and once I start accepting favors like that, the way things are, I'd feel . . ."

"Obligated to . . . pay him back?"

"Not that, exactly. Well, maybe something like that. How does a woman say no to a man she loves when he has literally saved her from ruination?"

"Not easily."

"I go at things so hellishly. You know me. I'm a fighter. I'd get possessive of Clifford's time and then demanding and want him all for myself, even though it would trap him. I care too much to do that to him."

Stephanie finished her cigarette in pensive silence and ground it out against a two-by-four. She pretended not to notice that Victoria's hands were shaking, and that she occasionally rubbed at her forehead as if it were aching. "Have you completely discarded the possibility of talking Eliot out of it? Directly, I mean."

"I've been thinking about it," Victoria answered almost apologetically, "but I hate to fly over there and leave you with the school to run by yourself. I keep thinking that if I were smarter I could find another way."

"Silly girl! I can run this place very well without you and you know it. I don't think you have much choice."

"Custer's last stand?"

Stephanie laughed. "Pretty much. Anyway, it's the perfect time for you to go to Austria. I would have only half a week alone, what with Thanksgiving."

For a moment Victoria considered the chances of making a deal with Eliot. At this point, anything seemed preferable to entrenching herself any deeper into Clifford's life. Taking her affairs back into her own hands despite the possibility of a disaster would be like telling Clifford that she made no demands of him, expected nothing in return, that she was her own woman, no matter what had happened between them. It seemed the only thing to do.

She chewed at a piece of straw, then clasped her hands about her knees and drew them up beneath her chin. Her eyes slipped out of focus. "Why does he have to be exactly what I want?" she asked hoarsely, more to herself than Stephanie. "Everything about him is perfect. His touch, his walk, his voice. When he holds me, Steph, I—"

When Victoria's forehead dropped forward to balance on her knees the pent-up tears of the past

snarling at her, its fangs bared. She placed it carefully back into the cradle and slowly turned to face a wide-eyed Stephanie.

"Get your coat while I throw some things into a suitcase," she said quietly. "I'm taking the first flight out."

For once, Stephanie behaved as if her sympathies were for Clifford. "But don't you think—"

"That's just it! If I talk to him I won't be able to think. This is a serious thing I'm caught in. And Brayntree . . ."

She dashed to her rooms, wondering how something so totally wonderful as her love for Clifford could cause so much excruciating confusion for so many people.

When Clifford screeched to a stop before the wrought iron gates of Brayntree the darkness was as menacing as his temper. He had missed dinner. He had come dangerously near to offending both his parents because he had refused to make a downpayment on the house for Faith and himself. It was his business, of course, they had said, but they just didn't understand what had gotten into him the last few days. He had winked at his mother and vowed he was in his mid-life crisis. She hadn't found it amusing. And, he was exhausted with worry about Victoria.

Except for the nightlights, Brayntree's main house appeared dark. Getting out of the car, Clifford sent a message bristling over the intercom mounted into an ivy-swathed pillar of gray stone.

"Who is it?" a cross reply popped back at him. "What's your business?"

"Clifford Pennington to see Miss Carroll. Is this Jack?"

Jack, if it were he, disdained to identify himself. "She ain't here."

Damn! "Where is she?" he demanded tersely, nursing visions of throttling Victoria. "Open this gate."

An irritated but nonetheless obedient sigh whistled over the static. "Awright, Mr. Pennington. But you'll have to see Miss Stephanie."

He could handle Stephanie Morris. "Just open this gate." The Porsche left an indiscrete mark of black rubber on the pavement.

"It's late," Clifford began as a clipped excuse of apology he felt obliged to offer when Stephanie wrenched open the door.

She was as tired as he was, and she stood resolutely blocking the doorway. Her lips were pursed as she shook her head at him.

He knew what she saw. He was haggard to his bones. Since she didn't move aside he slouched against the door frame, and his heavy jacket fell open to reveal a terry shirt instead of the starched business shirt and tie she obviously expected. She ran her eyes over his tan trousers and the tops of his shoes.

His eyes burned from lack of sleep, and tension had his jaw in a vise. "You've made your point," he drawled.

"Couldn't you have done this over the telephone?"

His laugh rippled mockingly. "I've been trying to do that for the last four days. Where is she?"

"Gone," came the succinct reply.

He chewed at the edge of his moustache with his lower teeth. *"Where?"*

"You know I can't tell you that."

"I'll find her anyway. You might as well."

Bridling, Stephanie retrieved a cup of steaming tea from the sideboard. She spooned in sugar, then lemon and pointedly refused to offer him any. He dismissed the rudeness.

"You'd better have long legs, Mr. Pennington," she said, her frown imperative, "because Victoria's out of the state." She sipped. *"Far* out of state."

Clifford shifted restlessly and, at her words, raked her with glinting eyes. He felt like tearing the room apart. But he prudently waited until she seated herself. When she crossed her legs he loomed over her like a titan.

"Now look, Miss Morris," he said gruffly. "I'm well aware of the fact that you don't care for me."

"Do you know why?"

He scowled. "No, I don't. And I really don't care."

The cup clattered in its saucer. "I suppose you don't remember a girl by the name of Darlene Kirzynski, do you?"

Clifford barely controlled his temper. He wiped a hand across his mouth then jammed it deep into his pocket. Slowly he let out his breath, checked. "Yes, I remember Darlene. Why?"

"She was a friend of mine." Stephanie's smile curved with frigid triumph, but Clifford guessed she wasn't as cool as she pretended. She absently picked up a pen and scribbled meaningless marks on a pad.

As disturbed as she was, he moved further across the room and listlessly stirred the fire. After placing two logs on the blaze he leaned to replace the poker.

"I love Victoria," Stephanie said levelly.

He spun about. The poker clattered noisily on the hearth. "And I love her. Look, Stephanie, for Victoria's sake we have to make some kind of peace between us. God knows I've made my share of mistakes. More than my share. One of them was Darlene. But what I feel for Victoria isn't a mistake."

"She's so fragile right now. You'll break her heart."

"I'm not going to—"

"You're already doing it!"

Inside his pocket Clifford's hand clenched into a hard fist. He understood the protective sympathies Stephanie cherished for Victoria; he cherished them himself. "You think only the fragile get their hearts broken? We all get our hearts broken." His words were hardly above a whisper. "Even you, Stephanie."

His statement was much too intuitive. Stephanie kept her blurring gaze fixed on her trembling hands. "My heart is not the issue here."

"I'm not so sure."

She finally looked at him, and he shook his head at her. His emotion was one of friendship, not anger.

"Don't let your own fear of loving influence Victoria. Don't make her afraid to take a chance. Love isn't just for the strong. Let her find her own way."

When he began flipping through the telephone messages she didn't try to stop him. He picked up the note pad she had been scribbling on and turned back its pages. Anyone could have figured out the numbers: the departure time in New York, arrival time in Vienna.

"Mr. Pennington?" she croaked.

"Is this the flight she took?" He tossed the pad to the desk with a ruffle of pages.

Stephanie's shoulders drooped with acquiescence. "You can see that."

He didn't move. "Austria? To try and do it all by herself?"

She nodded.

"So damnably proud," he muttered under his breath, angry.

She sat speechless as he dialed the airport and inquired about the next connections to Austria. When he replaced the receiver she clicked her tongue against her teeth. "It wouldn't do any good to try and persuade you to let her do this by herself, would it?"

Smiling at her, allowing his shoulders to straighten and his weight to shift equally to both feet, Clifford was anxious to get started. A small triumph slithered down his back. He wanted to lessen the distance between Victoria and him. Miles stretched between them, and a time of waiting until he could ask her to marry him. So he sighed.

"Not in the slightest, Miss Morris," he answered and rubbed his chin. "Not in the slightest."

Chapter Eight

Somewhere in the sentimental fringes of her mind Victoria had imagined that traveling to Europe would be romantic and breathtakingly exhilarating. Perhaps that was because she and Helen had spent long hours dreaming of sidewalk cafés in Paris, the Grand Prix at Freudenau and seeing *Die Fledermaus* at the Vienna State Opera House.

Or perhaps, she mused, the fascination of Europe was linked to a long-discarded girlish fantasy—the tall, mysterious prince wearing a white uniform with skin-tight trousers and his chest sparkling with decorations of valor who would sweep her off her feet in a magnificent whirlwind. Since the puzzle of the man had been solved in a most practical manner, and since he was an attorney with a moustache who tended to prefer blue jeans to trousers and whose chest was markedly bare of medals, she didn't have men on her mind when her train pulled into Innsbruck, Austria.

Innsbruck was the capital of the Tyrol and was one of the most beautiful towns of its size in the world. She was arriving at Innsbruck, naturally, at the wrong time of year, too late for the trade fairs and too early for the best of the winter sport competitions and music festivals.

But none of that mattered. She hadn't taken one of the most strenuous journeys in her life to go sightseeing and buy tourist trinkets. She would save Brayntree if she could, and if things went well maybe she could establish some type of relationship with a father whom she hardly knew and a stepmother she had never met.

Just before sunset Victoria stepped off the train in the city where Eliot was spending the winter with their father and Gretchen. According to Helen, Gretchen Redl had scandalized her close-knit family by marrying John Carroll—"one of those horrible Americans"—and John had scandalized them even more by taking up residence in Austria to help Gretchen run the *fremdenheim*.

Operating the modest guest house with its dozen beds and breakfast service surely couldn't be much of an undertaking, Victoria surmised. How many people would pass through here in a year's time? Or would be guests at the *fremdenheim?* True, the place was stunning, crescented by the sheer sides of the mighty Alps, a blue and white wall. But to her, a woman traveling alone, it was like coming to the end of the world.

Thank goodness she had finally managed to locate Eliot from the airport in Vienna. *Where was he?*

"Victoria!"

She saw him then, a pale, lanky man whose clothes were nondescript, and whose blond hair was almost hidden beneath a red and white ski cap. Eliot looked exactly like what he was: an artist, a sensitive, extremely talented young man, which was the reason Helen had insisted on sharing her worldly goods with him. John Carroll would let the impractical boy starve to death, she had said.

Waving to her stepbrother, Victoria watched him weave himself expertly between the straggling tourists who had been in Vienna shopping and sightseeing and had come back to their hotels burdened with armloads of wrapped parcels. Grabbing up her one piece of luggage, besides the tote slung over her shoulder, she trudged to meet him, praying that things would be cordial.

"I couldn't believe it after you called," he said and hugged her with more enthusiasm than she expected. He grinned down at her from his towering height. He was almost as tall as Clifford. "I tried to locate Father and Gretchen, but they're in Vienna and won't be back until late tonight."

Smiling tiredly, Victoria let him carry her suitcase. "That's all right. Forgive me for just . . . *coming.*" She shot him a sidelong glance, wondering at his cheerfulness. "I thought we needed to talk face to face about something this important."

"Wasn't the lawyer any good? He keeps me posted pretty well, so I thought he was doing his job."

"The lawyer was fine," she said softly.

Eliot gestured undauntedly toward his blue Fiat parked a distance away. "Well, we can talk about all that later. You must be exhausted. You look different."

That she loved Clifford couldn't show, she

thought, horrified. Giving her tongue free rein, she began chattering about her trip, her confusion over the complicated system of tipping, going through customs. She talked and talked and talked.

"Why didn't you fly in?"

Her mind was racing as she pulled on her gloves. She hardly heard his question when the high-pitched giggle of a child behind her caught her attention. She turned to see a married couple walking with their arms grasping at skis and sticks. The man was rather stout, plain-faced, and wore a strange-looking hat. Some would have called him ugly. Beside him, a small woman lugged her share of the burden. If she had been a bit more clever with makeup and hair-styling she might have been quite pretty.

"Do you think I can learn to ski in just five days, Papa?" asked the tiny cherub as she clung to her father's coattails and tried to match his big steps with hers, dragging her zippered bag in the dirty snow.

The spectacled man glanced back at her and paused. "Sure you can, kitten. When I was your age I cut quite a figure on a pair of skis, didn't I, Mother?"

Not hearing the mother's eager agreement, Victoria smiled at the adoring trust of the child. The small chubby hand reached upward to grasp her father's, but he, stooping, tossed her high on his shoulders in spite of his skis. She was a bundle of flashing red jacket and pants and white mittens and cap. Her gaiety sounded over the late afternoon landscape, making isolation wrap about Victoria's shoulders like a cloud of wet fog. The mother, with pride glowing in her eyes, didn't appear nearly so home-spun now. In fact, they were both incredibly fortu-nate, in no way plain, and extremely blessed.

When the father laughed a triumphant laugh

which took everything he possessed for granted, Victoria suddenly envisioned the scene of Clifford with his own daughter. His natural virility was only enhanced by the curly-headed moppet which scuttled across the floor toward the trap of his waiting lap. His large hands spanned the tiny middle as he laughingly held the baby above his head then lowered her to bury his face in the rounded tummy.

The infant crowed at his ferocious growl and tangled her dainty fingers in his hair. His yelp was predictable and perfectly fitting. In time this daughter would tame him in many ways and she would wrap his heart about her fingers without mercy until Clifford would wonder if there had ever been another life without her.

Oh, Clifford, Victoria mourned as she walked beside Eliot. *My sweet, sweet Clifford. You are haunting me. How I wish I could give you that.* But she never could. Faith Chambers would probably give Clifford his daughters. In her heart she feared it immeasurably.

"Vicky?" Eliot's voice came from a great distance.

Victoria snapped back to the harsher reality of her surroundings. "Oh, I'm sorry, Eliot. And don't call me that. You know I've always despised it."

"Beg your pardon, ma'am," he said, teasing, inclining his head. "I was asking you why you took the train from Vienna instead of flying straight on?"

"Hm? Oh, I just needed some time to myself. I had a lot of things to think about, and I figured the afternoon's ride would be good for me."

"Was it? Good for you, I mean."

She managed not to wince at his uncustomary curiosity. By now they were at his car, and he tossed her luggage into the tiny cluttered compartment along with two soft drink containers, some candy wrappers and a tattered copy of a Charles Bronson movie tie-in.

"As good as anything could be right now." She had no intentions of discussing her personal affairs with him. "Where is this Hungerburg Plateau?"

He glanced over his shoulders at her as if she should have known. "My dear, you are now at the pivot of Tyrolean tourism. The Hungerburg Plateau is up there." He pointed upward to a hill which overlooked the town. "Three thousand feet above sea level. It's wonderful up there. You'll love it. Of course, at the inn we only have beds and breakfast. But Gretchen runs a clean place. You'll be coming back down to the city a lot, so never fear. How long can you stay?"

She crawled into the car and laughed at him. "Not long enough to put much of a cramp into your lifestyle. I have to be back when my girls return from their Thanksgiving holiday. There are decisions I must make."

At the mention of Brayntree's possible sale Eliot grew subdued. He gave all his attention to driving up the twisting incline. Victoria, watching him, saw the indecision tracing its lines beside his mouth. If his intentions were wavering, why had he rejected her offer of a yearly allotment?

Eliot drove skillfully. Every fold and crevice of the slopes crowded thickly into the road, making abutments here, precipices there. Outside her window beyond the network of cables for the lifts, crawled the chain railway to one of the more lofty aeries a good seven thousand feet up. Ordinarily she would have been awed, but much of the majesty was lost to her now. She couldn't turn and place her hand on Clifford's arm and say, *Look, darling, isn't it lovely?* Beauty, she mused, was beautiful when it was shared.

Victoria found her room small but spotless and very quiet, one of the few with a private bath and which looked out over one of the truly marvelous scenes of the world. The chilly pinewood floor was scrubbed nearly white. A bright rug kept things from being completely Spartan. The furniture was solid pine, and one piece caught her eye, prompting her to kneel before it, to run her fingertips over the dark wood. It was an old chest with painted panels, a fine example of Gothic workmanship which wouldn't have been out of place in her own bedroom at Brayntree.

For her first evening in Austria Eliot's unpresuming nature was exactly the thing she needed. After a brief friendly chat in her room, he courteously presented her with a box of sandwiches and some dried fruit. He excused himself with the promise of treating her like royalty the next day.

Since royal favors had never appealed to her, and since she was practically asleep on her feet, she moved straight to the shower. Freezing, she dried herself and wriggled into her gown. On second glance the room began to tell her things, in the fraying edges of the furniture cushion, the small patch in the lampshade, even the clever repair job on the draperies. The bedspread, though neat, was worn and faded.

She crawled in between icy sheets. Gretchen's Austrian *fremdenheim* was hurting for money, she gathered. But she was too tired to think about it now. For the first time since she had slept in Clifford's arms, she breathed in the faint smell of soap in the pillowcase and drifted into a deep, dreamless sleep.

John Carroll had never liked being a father. And he generally wasn't all that fond of women. The one thing he absolutely couldn't resist—his classic flaw, he called it—was tackling something everyone believed was doomed to failure.

Helen Brothmeyer Carroll had been one of those impossible women with her matchless aesthetic taste and her impeccable reputation. Except, he hadn't been able to hold that challenge together. Not even after Victoria had been born. The frugal Austrian inn was another, involving not only a third marriage which everyone, including Gretchen Redl herself, said would never last. But the inn also demanded a clever manipulation of money.

True, the guest house wasn't a monumental business. Its collapse wouldn't shatter the world's economy. But Austria was where he was, and he was growing too old to start over again. His hair was thinning and beginning to gray. He hardly recognized the face in his mirror anymore. At the end of each day he was tired, very tired.

So he couldn't fail in this, he reminded himself now as he and Gretchen returned from Innsbruck at a half-hour past midnight. Eliot's share of Helen's estate would redeem this business venture; it would keep the business from being swallowed up by runaway inflation. He *had* to have that money.

"Victoria is *what?*" he demanded when Eliot met him in the lobby downstairs.

Eliot blinked his sleepy gray eyes in an attempt to wake himself. He had fallen asleep on one of the sofas. "She's here. Upstairs asleep. Called me from Vienna early in the afternoon."

John ran his hand through the thinning strands of hair, an unconscious habit. "Did she say what for? Did she bring the money? What the hell—"

The woman beside him touched his shoulder. Her face was partially obscured by a hat slightly out of fashion. Gretchen Carroll was average in almost every respect: height, weight, beauty, all except her disposition which was wonderfully congenial.

"Shh," she said and stepped to place an armful of parcels beside the reception desk. "Keep your voice down, John. You'll wake everyone up."

Letting his shoulders droop, Eliot frowned darkly at his father. "I didn't talk to Victoria about the money. If you want to know, ask her yourself."

"You're damn right I will! What room is she in?"

"Not now, John!"

"Father," Eliot curled his thin, artistic fingers about John's sleeve in an act of aggression he didn't often display, "I told her you'd see her in the morning."

John muttered something under his breath, but Gretchen smiled at him, soothing his ruffled feathers with a wifely pat. She drew him toward the stairs, and he absently followed, his thoughts elsewhere.

"In the morning is fine. Turn out the main lights, Eliot. Come to bed, John."

They dressed for bed in silence. The room was frigid, and it took all their stamina to manage buttons and hooks. Only when the lights were out and the blankets had chased the chill from his bones did John speak.

"I don't care what the girl says," he mumbled. "I was married to Helen. I know the kind of woman she was. She just loved to keep nest eggs—for a rainy day, as she put it. Victoria can afford to give Eliot his money, and I know it. It's not like Eliot doesn't have it coming."

Through the darkness Gretchen made a sound of disagreement. But she never openly argued with him, so she only said, "She's your daughter, John. Perhaps she needs more time."

"Time? What does Victoria know about time at twenty-two. *I* know about time. Besides—"

He didn't finish, and presently Gretchen asked, "Besides, what?"

"She never calls me Father," he admitted gruffly, as if it humiliated him to confess such a thing. "She calls me *John*. Helen taught her to call me John."

"She doesn't know you. Maybe if you treated her like a father she would think of herself more as a daughter."

John was unconvinced. He rolled over on his side of the bed and flung an arm out from beneath the covers. Cuddling herself to his back, Gretchen slipped her arm about his waist. He was grateful for her warmth and inched closer against her.

"She calls me John," he muttered again and soon began to snore.

Victoria dreaded going downstairs to breakfast and facing her father. Not because she hadn't seen him since Helen's funeral, but because they were, and always had been, strangers. The times they had been together had always been awkward, nerve-racking ordeals which left her spent and stricken with the conviction that she had failed him in some awful, unidentified way.

This morning she dressed with fastidious care, selecting the best pair of slacks she owned. She complemented them with a simple inexpensive sweater, but the scarf knotting about her throat bore a label from Cartier. When she shrugged into the Armani jacket which had always done her in good stead she realized she was shaking.

Nerves, she thought. And why did she give a hang what he thought of her appearance? Why was it important? She had no idea. It just was.

One last inspection in the mirror reassured her that she looked her best—smart, classically understated. Still, this wasn't the kind of breakfast where appearances would count. Power would count, power to persuade them to wait, to convince them there was a better way.

Punctually at eight, Eliot had said. It was now three minutes past.

Only one waiter served the entire dining room at the guest house. Breakfast consisted of a buffet of omelets, paper-thin slices of meat, several sugary confections and coffee fixed any way one could possibly desire it: black, spiced, mocha, *melange.* The guests ambled in at their pleasure, and though they were strangers, the isolation of the Alps infused them with the atmosphere of family. The dining hall bustled with infectious holiday banter.

Her father had returned during the night, Victoria was informed by the balding man at the desk as he peered over the top of his newspaper. He nodded toward a niche separated from the rest of the dining room by half-open French doors. When she tapped lightly on one of them, pushing it slightly more open, a soft German voice said to enter, please.

Victoria stepped inside. Past the window she glimpsed thin folds of gray mist enveloping the mountains. But sunlight already glinted through them like silver threads shot through a tapestry. The room was chilly; she shivered slightly.

From over starched napkins and coffee cups, three

heads lifted. As John Carroll folded his paper Victoria was as aware of the accents of rosewood furnishings as she was their polite rustle to welcome her. The chairs were polished rosewood, as were the sideboard and the portable cart which bore plates of food from the buffet. The same stark moderation, the same spotless sparseness which she had noted earlier, was evident here.

John Carroll's eyes brightened at the sight of his daughter. Arising in his practical Continental manner, he kissed her cheek as if he had seen her only the week before.

"You look absolutely beautiful, my dear," he complimented her and kept his hand on hers. "Isn't she pretty, Gretchen? I started half a dozen times to wake you up, Victoria, but Eliot told me you were worn out from your trip. Why didn't you call us?"

He stood properly straight in trousers which had once been an excellent pair of tweeds. His sweater, Victoria guessed, was handmade, probably by Gretchen. Though his graying hair was beginning to thin, he was still an extraordinarily handsome man, not looking his lean side of fifty at all.

As he always did, Eliot appeared fine and fit, blissfully unconcerned with mundane matters in his jeans and shabby sweater.

Gretchen Carroll was one of those moderately pretty women with an expression incapable of disguising her character. Her blue eyes were bright, highly intelligent, and she possessed the fine breeding which went much deeper than the unobtrusive yellow slacks and shirt she wore. Her smile glowed with warmth.

"Yes, she's lovely, John. But I expected her to be." Half rising, she drew Victoria down to a chair and bent near her, pressing Victoria's fingers to her cheek. An instant rapport surged between them when Victoria saw that Gretchen's hands were hard, knotted, irreparably ruined from years of misuse.

All through breakfast the obvious purpose of Victoria's visit was meticulously avoided. They behaved as if the unpleasant issue before them were an object in the center of the table which, if ignored long enough, might cease to exist. The time was spent laughing over meaningless anecdotes of Eliot and Victoria as children.

Eliot surprised Victoria by appearing more like a bystander than she was herself. Anything his father did or said was met with withdrawn silence. Was it possible, Victoria mused over the rim of her coffee cup, that Stephanie had been more right than wrong? That perhaps Eliot wasn't the true culprit at all, but John Carroll?

In a fatherly way, John cleared his throat and folded his thin fingers on the table. He said, in his most pontifical tone, "As much as we're delighted that you came to visit us, my dear, we can't put off talking about your reasons forever."

For interminable moments they all paused.

"Well," Victoria began, not relishing a verbal contest, "you know I'm desperate to save the school, John. For the past weeks I've tried everything I know to raise Eliot's half of the money. It seems impossible. Unless I sell, that is."

The flash of her father's teeth could hardly be called a smile. "Surely it can't be as bad as all that, dear. I was married to Helen, you remember. She was . . . a careful woman."

Victoria wisely refrained from blurting, *What's that supposed to mean?* "You may have been married to her, but you didn't know her, John. There is no money, I assure you. The school operates from month to month on what it can make. One bad year would wipe me out."

John wasn't crude enough to cause a public scene. For an instant his pipe was suspended over the vinyl pouch of tobacco he held until he was certain he had the attention of everyone. Then he gave the filling of it his thorough absorption, as he chose his words with extreme urgency.

"Perhaps you've overlooked something," he suggested coolly.

The pipe fitted between his teeth. He shifted to one hip to replace the tobacco in his pants pocket. "A trust fund you could depend upon?"

Beads of moisture began drizzling down the backs of Victoria's knees.

"An insurance policy?" he continued the insinuations and sucked a pale yellow flame into the pipe. He lowered it and braced his arms on the table, leaning forward so she couldn't possibly misconstrue his meaning. "Bonds, Victoria?" he prompted in a totally supercilious manner.

The whole atmosphere of the exchange changed abruptly from the pink glow of rosewood and cordiality to dampness and rotting mistrust. Gretchen plucked at a thread of the tablecloth with such viciousness that it would have to be mended. Eliot squirmed in his chair and repeatedly stirred at a cup of coffee which was nearly empty.

Rarely had Victoria felt so whipped. She had known much frustration, even defeat, but never this humiliating patronization which crushed her now. *He thinks I'm lying! My own father! He thinks I'm lying!*

In the past she had thought she possessed no feeling for John Carroll, one way or another. But now the beginnings of disgust sprouted in her mind.

She didn't want him looking at her with those condescending eyes. She didn't want him looking at her at all! Turning, she searched for Eliot. Her stepbrother had disappeared.

She scanned the lobby for sight of Eliot, beyond the French doors, past the reception desk, to the entrance of the guest house. She found him standing near the main doors, his slender back to them, talking to someone. He moved aside gesturing.

Victoria saw the man clearly. As unerringly as if she waved to him or called out, his eyes flitted coolly across the busy space. They collided with hers. For a scintillating moment she read . . . what? Relief? Then anger, a burning, smouldering fury. In a moment, however, the mask slammed into place over his features. He strolled toward the breakfast niche with an indolent stride which sent Victoria's senses reeling with shock. This was unbelievable!

Throwing one side of the French doors wide, he filled the space with the loose-jointed ease of a man who knows precisely who he is. After one glance at the pinched transparency of her expression, the edges of his mouth compressed a bit. He let his inspection absorb the stress about her shoulders, the startled injury of her posture.

"Hello, Miss Carroll," he said, deceptively pleasant.

Victoria quickly disguised her wonder at seeing him. She told herself that she didn't need to dart behind his back and wrap her arms around his waist like a child. She wouldn't be safer with his body between John and herself; he was one of them, he was on their side.

"Hello, Mr. Pennington," she breathed weakly.

Though Clifford wore a suit, he still managed—in his graceful, lanky way—to appear capable of most anything. Using this to his advantage, his dark brows drew together. He extended his acknowledgment across the table with a nod at John Carroll. The pipe threatened to dangle as John's jaw loosed. They exchanged the briefest, sparest of smiles.

As if by magic, Eliot appeared behind Clifford and broke the tension by explaining that Clifford had come with papers for his consideration, that this was a convenient side trip for some other pressing matter. Wasn't it lucky that the two were so conveniently located?

Victoria wanted to laugh hysterically. She wanted to yell at all of them, *"This isn't fair! Four against one isn't fair!"* But, of course she couldn't say that, and the dangerous moment was suddenly past. They would deal with this in a civilized fashion. The crisis would ebb like a wave falling impotently back out to sea.

At John's almost gushing insistence, they all settled around the table and ordered fresh coffee and inquired about Clifford's trip in what Victoria considered an inane charade. She refused to look at Clifford when he adjusted his chair directly across from hers. She didn't dare let him see her mistrust nor her gnawing uncertainty of where she stood with him now.

"So you have good news about the settlement?" beamed John. He smiled reassuringly at Gretchen's mounting nervousness.

Clifford tossed him an unreadable grin. "I hope you think so," he answered.

Beneath the table, Victoria uneasily crossed her legs. The rock-hard intimacy of Clifford's leg immediately pressed against hers. Her shocked stare, when it crashed into his, read nothing in his cool look. Smiling innocently, he pinned her calf between both of his—erotically demanding, unrelenting, warning.

A scalding flush crept up her neck. "I didn't know your practice was so widespread abroad, Mr. Pennington," she blurted the first thing which came to her mind. "I hope your trip is successful."

Not even the flicker of a muscle marred Clifford's serene discretion.

"Actually," he explained, including her father in the conversation, "it's a nice combination of business and pleasure." He lifted a brow at Victoria and smiled again. "And I anticipate success, on both counts."

The gold of Clifford's eyes wasn't smiling. It burned, blazing with the intimation of many things yet to be resolved between them. Victoria winced at the force of the undercurrents clashing between them.

John Carroll cleared his throat impatiently. "Before you arrived, Mr. Pennington," he said, "we were discussing the property settlement. You'll be happy to learn that Victoria has solved the problem for us. She's finally made her decision to sell the school."

Wrenching her foot free of Clifford's trap, Victoria rose from the table in alarm. She struck the edge of it with her hip. All eyes were riveted to her, and Eliot looked as if he would like to dash out of the room.

"You're wrong, John," she said dully. She leaned across the table toward her father. "I haven't completely decided yet. I . . . give me a little more time."

John's next words ended the conflict between father and daughter with the finesse of a blade between her ribs: the death blow—clean and sharp.

It wasn't only the words that felled her, but that he said them at all with such malicious coldness.

Ignoring the dangerous rustle of Clifford's body in his chair, John levelled his gaze at his daughter with grave intensity. "I'm afraid, Victoria," he said quietly, "that I insist."

She thought the remnants of her pride dissolved before her eyes. It melted like a piece of precious gold thrown heedlessly into a fire. How could he humiliate her before a man like Clifford? She sank to her chair with the slow motion of an old woman.

For a disbelieving space of time no one said anything. Once, Victoria thought that Clifford might come to his feet. But before he could react she wearily pulled herself to her own feet. With a resignation she had often observed in her mother she straightened her spine as much as possible. She lifted her chin with a noble dignity she didn't even realize she possessed.

"I'll find someone to make the appropriate arrangements," she said in a small voice.

She no longer belonged here. She wondered if she belonged anywhere as she began to walk away, her feet feeling like dead weights.

"You'll see," John called cheerfully after her. "It'll work out for the best, Victoria. It never was right for one child to have everything and for one child to have nothing."

Victoria didn't raise her voice when she turned to him. Hardly a muscle moved in her whole body. She stared at him with an expression frighteningly void of emotion, unless it was a flicker of cold pity. Without theatrics she said, "My mother owned Brayntree before she ever knew you, John. And you want the money for yourself, not Eliot."

John's embarrassed oath sent a shudder knifing

across the back of her shoulders. Vicious memories of him yelling at her mother flashed through her mind. She didn't need to look at him to know his nostrils were flared, that his knuckles were colorless with rage, and that he didn't love her and never had.

A chair scraped disagreeably across the waxed pine of the floor as she reached the door. Clifford's lazy voice cut through the drama with the impact of flooding a dark room with merciless light.

"Stay where you are, Victoria," he drawled with deadly menace.

Not turning, Victoria froze where she stood. As he stepped near her back the comforting scent of musk caressed her face. She drew it deep into her lungs as if it would somehow strengthen her enough to escape the hideous hatred in this room. Grateful for it, her head dropped forward.

"I can't help but say, Mr. Pennington," her father gritted his accusation nastily, "that I find this all highly irregular. Coming in here unexpectedly like this. And this obvious . . . friendship with my daughter. You're my son's counsel at law, remember. You're being paid to see to *his* best interests."

Victoria whirled about at the unfairness in John's words. Even from her vantage, Clifford's actions had never been anything but meticulously ethical toward Eliot. Though she had no vitality left to defend herself, she would have defended Clifford's integrity to her last breath. Her mouth opened to speak.

Clifford, however, faced the greed of John Carroll with a power Victoria was incapable of. He shifted his weight to one foot in a deceptive slouch.

"Then consider me off the case, sir," he said lightly.

"Agreed, by God!"

Eliot lurched to his feet. "No!"

John's composure suffered a bit from the attorney's refusal to be intimidated. He brushed his son's objection aside as if Eliot were a bothersome puppy. "Stay out of this."

To maintain his dignity John was forced to stand, facing Clifford. The line of conflict had been drawn with such virulence that Victoria was shocked to suddenly realize it didn't concern the property at all. It was a primordial duel between John and Clifford as men: It involved no words, no distinctions, nothing except the instinctual urge of one man to take and the other to defend.

John's face twisted with his struggle to regain his lost authority. But Clifford's command, though silently dignified, was uncompromising, overpowering. His very poise made John appear incompetent. Victoria stiffened with premonitions of disaster.

"Mr. Pennington is an honest man," Eliot said timidly. "We're not corporations arguing here. We're a family."

John snorted.

"Mr. Pennington knows this case, and he can help us come to the best decision," Eliot insisted, something he rarely did in the face of his father. "*I* filed the petition, and *I* want him to remain on the case."

In his excitement, Eliot had leaned forward over the table. His weight was braced onto his hands, his face flushed with determination.

The sight of him in a state of rebellion, restrained though it was, seemed to enflame John even more. "You fool!" he laughed at him. "The man doesn't care one whit about your petition. Where're your eyes, boy? He's after your stepsister's petticoat, not your interests."

Horror drained the strength from Victoria's body. She darted a miserable look at Gretchen, but the woman sat transfixed, as if the ugliness of the scene had sent her spinning away to a private place in her mind.

Thrusting out her hand in a reflex reaction to prevent herself further pain, Victoria cried out. Her voice was unbearably brittle. "You have no right—"

"I wouldn't say very much if I were you, daughter," John mocked.

Tears sprang into Victoria's eyes. Unknowingly she retreated a step. Wrapped in her own abject mortification, she was oblivious to what Clifford was doing. The tall man drew near John Carroll. The gold of his eyes darkened dangerously, hooding a tightly reined violence that John could only guess at.

"What kind of a father are you?" Clifford demanded. His words were gravely soft. "You pit child against child? For what? Money?"

John unwittingly gripped the back of the chair before him. His nails cut into the grain. "What do you know of fatherhood?"

Clifford's reply was tightly restrained. "I know what it is not."

"Well, let's talk about money, then. I know you understand that well enough. I've known men like you all my life, Mr. Pennington. Fat cats who never worry about anything except if the gas tank is full when they want it. Get off my back, man. Go back where you came from and play lawyer like you're being paid to do."

Victoria was so ashamed that she wanted to go to Gretchen and fold her arms tenderly about her and say she was sorry. For what? Because she, the child, had given birth to the father? Helplessly she pressed her fingertips against her mouth as Clifford stepped to a small piece of luggage he had brought with him.

Tossing the bag with light carelessness to the table,

Clifford snapped it open. They watched him with a varied mixture of emotions. He withdrew a brown leather book and bent over it, writing unhurriedly. In a moment the tearing of paper was heard throughout the deadly silence of the room.

"What?" Victoria began and stepped forward.

But Clifford had already thrust the blue paper into Eliot's hands. For a second the younger man's eyes moved across the check. "My God, Mr. Pennington!" he breathed. "I don't understand."

"I believe two hundred thousand is what you were to receive?"

Eliot choked in disbelief. His father deftly lifted the check from his trembling fingers.

"There's nothing to understand," Clifford replied. He tended to his luggage now without looking at anyone. He clipped the latch shut, then swept the zipper closed. "I'll send the proper papers for your signature when I return to my office." Then, glancing at John and smiling coldly, he lifted his brows. "The check's a good one, Mr. Carroll. Eliot won't have any trouble with it." He moved, then hesitated. With a meaningful look he added, "I suggest you spend it well. She owes you nothing now."

In the one area where John was most sensitive, Clifford had outguessed him. The battle was won. John knew it. He took a step forward, chagrinned. "Mr. Pennington—"

Something about the way Clifford held his head caused the man to freeze in his tracks.

Victoria stood watching dumbfounded, only beginning to realize what was transpiring. She took three steps toward her father, but Clifford closed meaningful fingers about her forearm. His words were low, controlled, adamant with authority. "Get your things, Victoria. We're leaving."

He began steering her toward the door, then paused to twist about as if he had just remembered something important. He bowed his head with genuine politeness. "It's been a pleasure meeting you, Mrs. Carroll. Perhaps again, under slightly less tense circumstances. Victoria?"

Before the German woman could reply, Clifford pushed Victoria forward ahead of him. She attempted to protest what was only beginning to make any sense to her. She knew that Clifford had given money to Eliot—two hundred thousand dollars. But where did that leave her now?

Her sputters of objection were an incoherent jumble as she found herself being guided toward the stairway. She was still in shock. "But I . . ." she began. "But—"

"But nothing," he said spinning her to face him. The need to hold her was so strong he had to clench his fists from grabbing her to his chest. His eyes raked over her haggard features, and his jaw set with a bitter oath to himself. He was honestly amazed at how a man like John Carroll could have sired someone as precious as Victoria.

"Do you want me to come up and help you pack?" he offered. "I need to make some phone calls if you can manage. We're catching the next flight to Vienna."

Her eyes continued to stare at him, glazed. She thought he looked oddly happy, considering the circumstances. Tiny lines criss-crossed over his cheekbones as he smiled down at her.

"You can breathe, Victoria," he grinned. "Everyone's doing it these days." Thinking she would fly back at him with a flaming retort, he frowned when she meekly nodded. "I had planned a dozen ways I was going to give your behind a good paddling when

I saw you," he said. "But I guess that can wait. Now be a good girl and hurry. For some reason, I don't particularly like this place."

Victoria stumbled obediently to the stairs, hardly able to think with the confused muddle she had once called her brain. The first thing she had to do was put her clothes back into her suitcase. The second thing was to get a grip on herself. She had to figure out what was happening to her carefully planned life. Clifford Pennington had actually written a check for two hundred thousand dollars! Eliot was paid off. And this man—the man whom she loved and who was engaged to marry Faith Chambers—was now half owner of Brayntree School for Girls!

Chapter Nine

The stormy thunderheads billowing beyond the wing of the jet a mile above the ground looked like some type of omen, an indication that her life was about to explode into a violent tempest. Nonsense, she thought; she didn't believe in omens. But if the frown creasing Clifford's handsome features was any barometer of the determination coursing through his musings she should prepare herself for a small hurricane.

She shouldn't have been surprised that Clifford reentered her life as he had. He had strolled in with a smile, but beneath the smirk was the no-nonsense, dead-aim expertise of a professional tracking his quarry. Not a bad analogy, she decided, since she was the quarry. And what part did John Carroll's behavior play in this scenario? A challenge to Clifford's pride? Some two-hundred-thousand-dollar annoyance to be dealt with only because John or-

174

dered him to back off? She couldn't accept that. She couldn't have mistaken Clifford's sympathy for her in that horrible room.

As for John Carroll, he defied any rational solution. She was still too numb to visualize what her new relationship with Clifford entailed, either: ensnared quarry or a highly expensive troublespot.

"Are you okay?" From his aisle seat Clifford stirred in an attempt to fit himself into the small space. Mumbling a curse, he braced one cramped leg against the seat in front of him and observed her with fixed, unsmiling interest.

The shaft of sunlight shooting across Victoria's lap was hardly wider than a needle. Idly, she poked her finger across its glittering path.

"I don't know," she answered him honestly. "I would like to scream and cry 'Why did he do that to me?,' but I don't even have the strength to weep. I think I understand a little better why my mother couldn't live with him. I can't even say I'm really surprised that he tried to use Eliot and me." Her hands refused to keep still. "I think . . ."

"Go on."

"This sounds awful, but I think I don't care if I never see him again. Do you think that's awful?" She squinted at him through an uncertain frill of lashes.

For a moment he pondered, and she had the distinct impression he was thinking not of her, but John. He smiled.

"I think . . ." He lifted a finger to touch his moustache. "I think you'd be pretty surprised at what I think."

Victoria's head dropped wearily against her seat, and she peered at the jet turbine which appeared to be effortlessly hanging them in the sky. "Nothing about you surprises me anymore, Pennington," she changed the mood of the conversation. "You really outdid yourself by writing that check. I haven't the faintest notion of how I'll pay you back."

Chuckling, he teased, "I'll think of something."

Her eyes flew open. His jibes were the last thing she wanted. "Don't be crude. I'll pay you back, and you know it. Every miserable penny."

Thinking he had never known a woman as fascinatingly proud as she, even at this deplorable period of her life, Clifford inclined his dark head toward hers until his breath ruffled stray wisps of her hair. She sat unmoving, suddenly hypnotized by it, needing it, wishing she were not too proud to take his fingers in hers and crush them, to admit that she was scared to death.

"Do you think we should thrash that out now?" he asked. "You've taken a pretty hard lick, Victoria."

"I've taken them before. It won't kill me."

"Not like this one. At least give it time to stop bleeding."

She risked a skeptical glance. "How do you know what I've taken? Especially what I'm thinking?"

Disregarding her energetic flash of resistance, Clifford tucked his head even lower. His forehead leaned comfortably against hers. "How can you love me, Victoria, and not understand that my feelings are inseparable from yours?"

Shocked, her lips parted involuntarily. "I never said I—"

"When John hurt you, darling, he hurt both of us."

Clifford's sympathy was a physical thing as he stroked her face and pushed a whimsical wave behind her ear. She fought an overwhelming urge to drop her head to his shoulder and tell him to just take care of everything, that she was exhausted with fretting over money and wills and inflation. The recollection of Faith Chambers' clear, trusting eyes made her shake her head free of his caresses.

"Please don't call me darling. I know you don't mean anything by it, but right now I'm too . . ."

"Too what, sweetheart?" he urged huskily, then tightened his mouth at her flashing grimace. "Okay, okay." He held up his hand. "I'm not playing fair, I know. We'll declare a truce. I swear I'll be good."

She raked his face with dark-eyed suspicion. "What do you mean, a truce?"

"Just for today. Everything unpleasant is off limits. That means John, the school, and," his humor sharpened, "even that vile little brushoff on your answering device."

Her lips curved into a pout which, in spite of the grimness of the circumstances, was delightfully charming. She assumed a deprecating air. "I'm not good at turning off my problems, Pennington. I cherish problems. I *thrive* on problems. I drain every drop of misery I can from them." She looked at him blankly. "Waste is a sin."

Clifford laughed. "Be a masochist, then." He consulted his wristwatch. "But for the next . . . seven hours you may not talk about it. You'll let me pamper you exactly like I want to, and we'll enjoy Vienna together. We'll wander around and see the sights like goggle-eyed tourists and I'll buy you coffee at Demel's. We'll spend the night at the Sacher hotel. Then you can worry and pace the floor all night if you want to."

Victoria's eyebrows flew mistrustfully upward. *"We'll* spend the night?"

Like a foiled protagonist in a play, he touched the heel of his hand to his forehead. "You wish me to give up sleeping, too? You've already cost me any semblance of peace of mind."

Her fingers flicked. "Your sense of humor is really quite nasty, Clifford."

"Well," he said lazily, grinning at her bristling frown, "since you feel that way I suppose I'll have to get you a separate room. But if you despise waste so much, throwing away a night in Vienna is one of the great sins of all time."

"You know what I meant. Quit looking like a misused hero."

Clifford's facetious groan trailed off into a sensual, throaty growl. Shifting to one hip, he held his hand suspended for a moment, some inches above her knee. "Oh, hell," he breathed and let the hand fall limply to his own knee.

His not touching her caused her to react more violently than if he had. A current shot straight to her stomach and radiated downward to become a low, aching throb.

"Clifford," she choked, "I'm not being coy. I'm too messed up today to fight off a barrage of passes."

"I didn't touch you."

"No," she sighed, "you didn't. But you know exactly what you did do. I can't afford any more mistakes in my life right now."

He started to object to the word *mistake,* but she interrupted him. "If we're going to make it through this day, no touching, no wheedling, no . . ." Both hands lifted to the sides of her head. "No . . . *anything.*"

Clifford was silent for so long she turned to see what he was doing. He was leaning back in his seat, and his sidelong gaze was slowly traveling from her crossed knees, over the swell of her thigh, the faint curve of her belly, her waist, up the swelling slope of her sweater. Finally, with nervewracking masculinity, he stopped at her mouth.

Her teeth ground together. "And will you stop looking at me like that? For pity's sake, Pennington, you'll have me in hysterics before the day is half over!"

His laugh was deep and enormously contented. He slumped very low on his spine. "Oh, my lovely Victorian Victoria. You can slap my hands, and I'll keep 'em in my pockets. You can bite my head off, and I'll even keep my opinions to myself. But no power on earth, not even that vicious temper of yours," he shot her a challenging smirk, "can keep me from looking. That much is still free."

Even in his playful, teasing frame of mind, Clifford Pennington would do as he pleased. Arguing would only result in weakening what reserve she still had left.

"Nothing is free," she ended the conversation.

"Remember that," he murmured.

Victoria was certain, as she hurriedly fished in her purse for her lipstick, that she wouldn't forget. She needed him today—his companionship, even the undressing looks he gave her, especially the blatant desire etched on his face. Somehow it healed the pain of being rejected by a father who should have loved her. What would she do if she reached the point where she couldn't live without Clifford?

So, one whole day of her life was spent strolling by Clifford's side in a city famous for its pleasurable charm; a European fairyland where nothing was too trivial to talk about; a capital where holiday faces pressed against the thick windows of buses to peer at them as they passed; a place where nearly everyone carried a camera, where dreams and images made it possible for them to survive a war nearly four decades past.

It was the coldest, brightest of sparkling days. Together they gazed at the Danube rippling past, icy blue. Neo-Gothic spires pierced the sky, and the shops in the Kohlmarkt bristled with elegance. As she stared up into the face of Pallas Athena before the Parliament building the selfish demands of John Carroll began to blur. Before the masses of noble statues decorating the Neue Burg Palace she found herself forgetting the cruel twist of her father's lips and memorizing, instead, the strong backs of Clifford's hands, the fine, wispy covering of sun-bleached hair. She studied the competent network of muscles cording his neck when he turned aside and the exquisite perfection of his ears, the furls of hair ruffling on his collar. How irredeemably she was falling in love with him!

While standing near him, even the noisy clamor of the city took on its own particular sort of enchantment. More than once she caught him standing perfectly still, studying her.

"Stop that!" she scolded him on a filmy thread of protest.

"I'm taking pictures," he grinned.

"You don't have a camera."

He shrugged. "I don't need one. Know what I mean?"

Yes, God help her, she knew what he meant.

The day passed much too quickly. They lunched, and the afternoon skimmed by on racing silver wheels. The habit of smiling at each other increased until it was more like a time-lapsed trance. She forgot to protest when he began taking her arm and drawing her beside him until his hip rubbed familiarly against hers when they walked.

"You're perfect," he said once and slipped his arm about her waist. In a natural caress his hand settled low on the slope of her hip.

"You're breaking the rule," she warned him with an odd lack of conviction.

"Damn the rule," he retorted and removed his hand. But he grasped hers and slipped it intimately into the pocket of his jacket, burying it deeply to press against the bones below his waist. She felt the powerful stretch and pull of his stride. For a moment they were as closely connected as if they were one, not two.

Her nerves stung. "What are you doing to me?"

His breath blew a crisp stream of vapor when he chuckled. "Nothing compared to what I'd like to do," he said and grimaced when she snatched her hand from the pocket.

"Oh look, Clifford!" Victoria exclaimed as she bent over a glass-topped counter in the Karntnerstrasse. It was late in the afternoon, and they had bent over innumerable counters this day. Pointing, Victoria directed Clifford's gaze to the back of the showcase where, behind myriads of glass and silver treasures, perched a daintily crafted figurine in goldleaf—a girl in the superlative garb of the Rococo period, her arms uplifted in the graceful position of the minuet.

Wisely noting her interest, the sober-suited owner, a woman of about fifty whose practical shoes perfectly matched the chignon twisted at the nape of her neck, quickly came forward and nodded her

approval of the fräulein's taste. She smoothed the
waist of her skirt and related, in such dreadful
English that Victoria could hardly comprehend it,
the history of the beautiful piece. Withdrawing it
from the case with solemn care, she paused and
twisted a mechanism at the bottom. She placed it
upon the glass top, then stood back with buxom
pride.

The gleaming figure twirled left, then right, spinning to the lilting melody of a waltz. Entranced,
Victoria leaned nearer. From his distance Clifford
hardly noticed the charm of the figurine; he was
much too absorbed with the wonder of Victoria's
delight. Over her head he met the eyes of the buxom
woman. The smile they exchanged was in complete
agreement; the young woman was breathtakingly
lovely and he was lucky to have her.

Reaching back in an absent gesture, Victoria
placed the tips of her fingers on Clifford's arm, the
unconscious mannerism of a wife sharing with a
husband. "See?" she exclaimed. "It plays Strauss!"

Half turning, she smiled with the most artless
happiness Clifford had ever observed. He bowed
from his waist in princely amusement and stepped
into her. Lifting her hand from his cuff by the tips of
her fingers, he drew her from the showcase and
proceeded to turn her in a graceful pirouette to the
rhythm of the waltz.

From behind the counter the woman laughed a
rich, gutteral compliment and called out in German
to random observers standing nearby. Her words
needed no interpretation. People drew nearer and
watched with rapt interest.

His lips curving beneath the brush of his moustache, Clifford grinned down at her. His eyes never

relinquished her shining ones. "I think they expect a performance, little one," he murmured.

She protested softly, laughing up at him. "But, Clifford . . ."

One of his large hands spread firmly at the small of her back. "When dancing," he insisted, "the man is king."

She shrugged pleasantly, teeth sparkling. "Long live the king."

By now everyone was bewitched by the tall handsome American who dared to waltz with his pretty young sweetheart in the crowded aisle of a Viennese novelty shop. They tossed encouragements to them and made more room by pressing against the walls. One woman, with a gurgling cry in French, took their picture. The flashbulb popped, and Victoria blinked. Clifford continued swirling her in a skillful pattern until the music slowed, then gradually came to a stop.

The entire performance lasted no more than two minutes at the most, but Victoria's uplifted face glowed pink. She had no idea of how lovely she appeared to him. When he finished the dance at the far end of the aisle he lifted her hand gallantly to his lips. The customers broke into a crackling applause.

Embarrassed then, Victoria ducked her head, flushing. She kept her eyes lowered as he said something to the beaming shopkeeper.

"You didn't!" she protested when the pleased woman placed the wrapped music box into her hands, together with a hearty *t'ank you* in English to the generous American man.

"You're such a lovely couple," she congratulated them. "You will have a dozen beautiful daughters like yourself, no?"

Averting her eyes, Victoria shook her head, anxious to escape such indulgent interest from strangers.

"Ah," soothed the woman, thanking Clifford again for his purchase, as if she were proud of having played a part in one of the great romances of all time. "In time," she encouraged. "In time."

"You shouldn't have bought this," Victoria scolded once they stepped into the bite of the afternoon's wind.

"One never tells the king what to do with his money," Clifford warned, teasing. "Only at the peril of losing his head."

"Well, your majesty, this subject most certainly does. You musn't keep doing things like this. First the money to Eliot—God only knows how that will turn out—now this! How much did it cost?"

Clifford spun her about by the shoulders and arched one disapproving eyebrow. "Didn't your mother ever teach you it's bad manners to ask how much a gift cost? My, my Victoria." He shook his head dolefully. "At times you absolutely amaze me."

"My mother taught me that a proper lady doesn't accept anything but the most platonic of gifts from a gentleman."

He sniffed. "An old, out-dated tradition of the South. It means nothing."

"Oh! Just forget I asked."

He chuckled and tucked her hand through his arm with outrageous flair. "Thank you, love. I fully intend to."

After that Victoria trod more softly with him. From time to time she glanced down at the wrapped parcel to make sure he had really done it. It was the most precious gift she had ever received. A dear, dear memory was wrapped in that brown paper, she told herself. She didn't think there would be many days when she didn't take out the lovely gold figure and play the waltz and remember him smiling down at her as they danced to Strauss.

By the time they strolled through Belvedere Palace garden and peered up at the six sculptured musicians, the wind whistled with dusky melancholia. Snow covered the statues' gray stone faces. They peered down with sightless eyes, and their instruments caught the lowering rays of the sun as if they, too, were cold.

During the last hour the amusing witticisms Victoria and Clifford had laughingly volleyed between them had dwindled like the music box in the shop. At times he had loomed beside her, woodenly thoughtful, his fists bunched deeply into his pockets as if the increasing chill were hurting him. Now, when Victoria gazed up at the poignancy on one of the sculpted faces, she half turned, seeking his opinion.

The golden eyes gazed longingly into hers. The familiar thread of unspoken communication spun out between them. She stilled, her hand outstretched.

"I'm kissing you," he said after a moment. "Can't you feel me kissing you?"

When he touched her she started. He placed the tip of his finger on the cold center of her lower lip, and she stood enraptured. As he traced the finely-drawn curve she held her breath, and her lip began to quiver.

"Can't you feel it here?" he murmured. "And here?" He paused at the delectable edge of her mouth.

She could no more play coy than if he held her foiled against a brick wall. "Yes," she said inaudibly.

"Then tell me you love me," he said, totally without warning. "I've waited for you to say it for a long time. All my life."

Tearing her eyes away, Victoria kicked blindly at the fluff of snow clinging to the toe of her shoe. Hadn't she secretly craved this moment? Didn't she need for him to make this demand so she could actually say the words? Yet saying them made a woman so vulnerable. It could be a rug to rake all the problems under. And she couldn't rake Faith Chambers under the rug simply because she loved him, nor the enormity of his generosity of writing out the check to Eliot.

"I don't want to make things more difficult than they already are," she replied, hedging.

"But you do love me."

His persistence genuinely frightened her, the fear of seeing herself at the depths of her own roots. Ever so slightly she gazed past his head, since he already read her much too well.

"Yes," she finally whispered as inaudibly as before.

"Look at me, Victoria."

They were standing in a terribly inconvenient place. All around them people were bustling. Mothers carried bundled babies back to warm houses, and other scurried with bulging shopping bags. Teenagers shaped snowballs and hurled them with indecipherable taunts before they had to go in for the day. Old men discussed unimportant things with great fervor as they stamped their feet to keep warm.

Ignoring all this, Clifford opened one of his arms, then the other. When he drew her aside to a projecting base of stone she didn't protest. She let his mastery envelop her. Images of them together yearningly and inseparably entwined flashed through her mind. As if he could see the erotic abandon of her thoughts, she flushed.

"Now," he said very gently as he leaned against her with his weight, pressing her back against the stone. "Tell me again."

Eyes brimming, she nodded. "Yes."

He took her lips with remarkable ease.

After a moment he muttered, "We're so good together, Victoria. So good." His mouth hovered only inches above hers. "I want you. *I want you.*"

The palms of her hands were pushing hard against his chest now. "But I can't let it happen," she whimpered. "I told you before."

"Then don't repeat yourself," he said to the precise tip of her nose and bent his head again.

Victoria reluctantly accepted his kiss. She told herself it was a fitting end to a day which had begun with utter insanity. But even a chaste kiss in a place as public as this one rattled her. She averted her face in an attempt to placate him with a fleeting peck on her cheek.

"Don't do that," he groaned, refusing the proffered cheek and grasping her head forcefully between his hands. As he repeated her name over and over in some private, tormented litany, he rained breathy kisses over her nose and her eyes, across her forehead and into her hair.

Though Victoria steeled herself to keep from responding to this open assault, the vulnerable exposure of Clifford's need battered through her ingrained defenses of social behavior. Her arms furled about the column of his neck. Her hands, acting of their own accord, became buried in the thickness of his hair. She brought his face down to hers with a hunger she rarely showed him and stood high on the tips of her toes.

Her quick darting tongue enflamed him as he fastened his mouth to hers. The surge of desire which bolted through him drove him hard against her, and he felt her trembling.

"Let's get out of here," he said between kisses.

It was when Victoria slipped her hands beneath his jacket, groping for the hard certainty of his back, that the stunning interruption made them remember where they were. The snowball smashed on the stone above their heads with the ringing impact of a shout. The singsong call which accompanied it was, Victoria thought, French.

She and Clifford hastily released each other to find at least five clear-skinned, dark-haired young boys grinning and going through the ridiculous mime of a lover pining away for his lady. One boy swept off a cap and bowed low in giggling admiration for Clifford's daring. Another, clasping a hand on his heart, dropped to one knee. The other hand flung out toward Victoria as he warbled a terribly off-tune ballad. She was sure the words were unrepeatable.

Having made their point, they scuffled among themselves, shouting at one another over the success of their conquest. They began sauntering away, their arms slung proudly over the shoulders of each other.

Clifford's first mistake was in surrendering to his temptation to scoop up a handful of the damp snow. With the skill of a veteran fighter of their age, he swiftly rounded it into a sphere. The weapon went hurtling into the back of the youth's head who had so fancifully doffed his cap. Having just replaced it with a swagger, he now found it knocked rudely off his head. He spun about, amazed and open-mouthed.

"Clifford!" Victoria exclaimed. She had never seen such a rashly frivolous side of him.

The older man's challenge to the boys exceeded any boundary of languages. Without hesitation, they eagerly took up the dare. Clifford's second mistake was in misjudging their skill in such a battle. As Victoria stood back, uncertain of whether she should go to Clifford's rescue or be delighted that he was in the process of getting his comeuppance, they barraged him with snowballs.

The contest was no contest at all. Clifford, if he did nothing else, accepted his defeat nobly. Dozens and dozens of snowballs landed all over him in a furious pelting. Only when he folded his arms over his head and yelled, "Enough, enough, enough!" did the boys slacken their assault.

As he stood serenely brushing the snow out of his hair and fishing it from the neck of his jacket, two of the boys, grinning, sidled forward. One even went so far as to extend his hand in a respectful handshake of congratulations that Clifford had dared to take them on.

With a mutual truce declared, the inevitable attempts to converse were launched. That, however, ended in a worse disaster. Among laughing shrugs of confusion, evidently deciding that fighting was better than talking any day, the boys waved goodbye and trotted off to tell everyone about the remarkable encounter they had just had with a "foreigner."

"Well, what am I supposed to say after that?" Victoria asked as he happily folded her hand over his arm and started walking her back to the rented car. "Hail the conquering hero?"

Clifford, his hair beginning to cling to his head in a

mass of moist waves, laughed down at her. "Defeat with honor, I think," he retorted. He bent to kiss the crown of her head.

"I learn more about you with each passing day," she mused as she matched her steps to his.

"I can teach you more, if you're inclined."

She ignored his suggestion. "From the waltz to the war, Clifford. I declare, what would your students say if they could see the dignified professor bested by less than half a dozen boys?"

But Clifford's thoughts had already diverted to more pleasant subjects, to the memory of how she had returned his kiss only minutes earlier. "If you were the prize, my darling, they would probably say 'Hang in there, guy. More power to you!'"

She smiled. Inwardly, though, she marveled at the quickness with which he was changing. He had defended her to her father's face, and now he had taken on a boisterous group of boys. What, she wondered, had he said to Faith?

Chapter Ten

The Sacher hotel was all baroque and gilt and plush scarlet and gold, as elite as its reputation was prolific. As Victoria tried to absorb everything at once since this would probably be the only time she would ever see it, she moved from one gorgeous oil painting to another. It never occurred to her to question why absolutely everything, from the paintings to the surroundings of rich mahogany and fresh flowers, pleased her. She only reserved a portion of her mind for Clifford's reactions; when he particularly liked something, she found it more satisfying than before. If he wearied, she was quick to turn away.

"This is . . . very Viennese," she said a bit shyly, gesturing at everything in general.

Clifford chuckled indulgently. "One thing I like about you, Victoria, you're so original."

"Shut up," she retorted and smiled with the scolding congeniality of a lover.

They were walking into the discreetly lighted bar after dinner. It seemed ridiculous that she would even consider marring the safe spell which had ensnared them the last hours. She should be practical and realize that her memories were valuable, that they could remain intact even if he never touched her again. She should leave well enough alone and let him continue lacing his strong fingers through hers, as if they could afford to be as carefree as high school sweethearts. They should live for this moment alone, she thought.

But, since she wasn't entirely practical, she gazed absently at a tall, stylish woman strolling into the bar on the arms of an impeccably dressed man and said, "The seven hours are up now, Clifford. We have to talk."

Holding her chair for her, then taking his own, Clifford smoothed back his hair and searched through the hubbub for the waiter. He tossed him a signal. "I thought," he replied, "that you might be magnanimous enough to not bring up unpleasantries."

"I'm not generous about some things."

"And *that*," he grinned devilishly, "is one of the great regrets of my life." At her threatening glare he sobered. "Ah yes, well, what do you want to talk about?"

"Do we have a choice?" she clipped briskly. "Faith, naturally."

"Mmm."

She had hoped he would tell her everything without her having to appear shrewish and extract it from him. Obviously he had no intention of being cooperative. The sting of anger made her talk too rapidly. "I wish I didn't even want to know. I wish I were capable of great selfishness so I didn't care."

The waiter, placing their wine before them, smiled his sterile, unseeing courtesy and stepped tactfully from the table. Grateful, Victoria slumped back on her spine and waited. She could feel Clifford arranging the order of his thoughts as he paid for their drinks. Presently he, too, leaned back, but he remained silent. Finally, thinking he was being unforgivably dense, she blurted out her question.

"Did you tell her about me?"

"No."

She felt like an orphaned child—slapped, rejected, kept in ignorance. "I see," she said coolly.

"No, you don't." He sipped, sighed a little and replaced his glass on the table. As he spoke he rubbed the stem of the glass. "In defense of myself, I must tell you that I let myself get inveigled in this . . . engagement because my life wasn't going anywhere. I was raised to believe that everyone's life should *go somewhere*. I had as many degrees as I could possibly use, a job that was too easy. The class at the college was simply a cure for boredom."

"You have your book," she threw in without thinking.

He moistened his lips. "Who wants to write a book? Anyway, I think my parents were beginning to panic."

"About what? That you'd wind up being a spinster?"

He shot her a smirk. "Something like that. Look, it wasn't Faith's fault that . . . well, that I met you. I don't want to hurt her, Victoria. We don't love each other, and she was willing to give it all a go, knowing that. We're friends. I want very badly to keep from hurting her."

"Do you think I do? Heaven knows, I've tried to protect her interests in this—"

His words were low, lethal. "This *affair?*" he supplied.

Her lashes fluttered to the rising color in her cheeks. She shook her head as if she were tired. "That's a cruel word."

Clifford hated to explain himself. Being in love imposed certain obligations, and he wasn't sure, at this moment, if he were capable of fulfilling all of them. "I simply told Faith I didn't want to get married. It . . . didn't seem right to tell her about us just then."

"And?"

"She asked if we couldn't talk about it again, after I'd had time to think it over."

Her violently mixed feelings seemed intolerable. She both sympathized with him and felt resentfully slighted. Behaving unfairly didn't matter at all, so she flung her words at him and pushed her glass from her in a gesture of finality.

"In the meantime," she said tightly, "you figure you can have a nice little fling with me. I hate to disillusion you, Clifford, but I'm a bit old-fashioned, in spite of the fact that I—"

"Fell in love with me."

"No! I mean, yes, but no . . . oh, damn you, Pennington! Your colossal selfishness never ceases to flabbergast me. You want it all—Faith's understanding and my . . ." She couldn't bear to finish.

The bar was so dark that candlelight cast gold highlights through his hair. They lent him a strikingly wicked look, and when he grinned in the middle of her serious, heartfelt discussion, she wished she were capable of causing a terrible scene. Perhaps if she slapped his face and stormed from the room he would take her seriously!

"Why are you staring at me?" she snapped caustically.

"I wasn't staring. I was thinking about your mother."

At the mention of Helen Carroll, Victoria felt the fight dissolve in her, like salt in the rain. Her forehead dropped forward onto the palm of her hand and she smoothed away the furrows. The deep intensity of her love for him was frightening.

"I think she would have liked me," he said softly.

"Why?" she asked without raising her head.

"Because I love you."

Her lower lip began, suddenly, to quiver. She bit it, which only made her look as if she were about to break into unmendable pieces. "I wish she were here. I need her so awfully."

"Because of John?"

"Because of John, because of the confusion in my life right now, because there is no clear cut right or wrong."

Sitting there, in the middle of all those people, most of whom didn't even speak a language she could comprehend, Victoria wished she could tell him that she would love him until the day she died. But she didn't know what he would say to such a confession, especially since he hadn't stood up to his family like a champion wielding a sword and said, "This is how it will be."

Like a petulant child she said, "Does all this make *me* the other woman? Or Faith?"

"That's not fair, Victoria."

"Well, you know what they say. Everything's fair in love and war."

Trying to hide his irritation because he couldn't control this situation, Clifford rubbed at the back of his neck. "I think we're having the war part of it now," he remarked bleakly. "I'm trying too hard. We're back to square one."

"What do you want of me? To admit I'm jealous? All right, I'm jealous and I hate it. Perhaps I can learn to smile while you blithely go your way, playing the all-powerful male who keeps everyone happy—Faith, your mother, the whole world."

"Everyone except you?"

"You want my happiness on top of all that? Oh, Clifford!" She looked away but knew that he leaned across the table, furious.

His words were harsh and grating. "I *want* you to look at me when you talk, damn it!"

Her brown eyes flashed, "I don't think I like what I see when I look at you, Pennington!" Instantly, she regretted her words.

"You rather liked what you saw when I stepped into that fracas with your father, my darling," he drawled.

He couldn't have struck her harder if he had doubled her up with the force of his fist.

Her smile was cold, dull and withdrawn. "I see," she said. *Why were they saying these horrible things to each other?* "So you thought you would buy yourself a two-hundred-thousand-dollar playmate? Well, I can hardly say no after that, can I? It puts my old-fashioned ideas back somewhere in the Dark Ages, at least. Congratulations, Clifford, you hold the winning hand."

He rose from his chair with the aristocratic dignity of a prince. She wished, in her grief, that she had bitten her tongue before voicing such hateful, unkind words. She wanted to grab his hands and kiss them and tell him she was sorry.

"You're mistaken, my love," he said, deadly quiet. "I haven't won. I've lost. And the funny thing is, I'm not exactly sure what."

He turned and walked out of the bar. She couldn't believe he would leave her like that. Fumbling in her purse, she placed some bills down upon the table, not looking, not caring. She walked after him as steadily and as dignified as she could without prompting heads to turn and gawk at her. By the time she reached the lobby he had requested his room key. With a weary, taxing stride he moved toward the elevator.

Victoria didn't follow him further. She didn't think she could. With dry, aching eyes she watched his elegance as he turned. As if they were joined but stretched apart with excruciating pain by some giant, unseen torture rack, his gaze met hers. She had never before seen the kind of anguish which now clouded his eyes.

I didn't mean to hurt you! her mind was screaming at him, but of course, he couldn't hear.

The elevator door swept smoothly shut. The delicate thing which had joined them was callously snapped in two, cleanly, no blood, no broken bones. Somehow her feet carried her to a chair and she sank down into it. Who reached out first when pain was equally divided? she wondered. Was it fifty-fifty? Or was it more like sixty-forty? What did pride have to do in the matters of love, anyway? She didn't know.

When she opened the door to her own room and stared at its emptiness, Vienna seemed ugly and unforgiving. She hated it. She hated the room. She hated herself, and she hated that virulent male strength that kept Clifford so above, seemingly without torture.

She thought, *I'll lie down and cry myself to sleep*. But even the solace of tears betrayed her when they wouldn't come. She lay staring at the dark interior of the room listening to the rustling of unfamiliar sheets when she tossed. Somewhere near the hour of midnight her hatred of herself grew indistinct. She knew she would go on living. Even if she hated many things and she lost Clifford, she would go on.

At last she slept.

Victoria came awake instantly aware of everything that had happened the evening before. Her mind, weary from lack of sleep, was peculiarly clear. Groping for the lamp beside the bed, she switched on the light. Two-thirty. Oh Lord, what now?

Slumping back against the headboard, she clutched the bedspread about her shoulders and grimly listened to the clamor of her own thoughts. She knew, in the honesty of the darkness, that she must go to Clifford. She had to repair what had been broken.

Her room, which had been large until the bathroom had been added, bristled with chill. The heavy curtains were drawn and a rug covered the floor, but she shivered as she made her way to the shower. Her teeth chattered as she scrubbed herself mercilessly, catching small, choking breaths. Toweling herself until she was tingling with revived energy, she skittered to her suitcase which lay open on a vanity stool beside the bed.

For a moment she turned aside to inspect her reflection in the mirror, criticizing the satin flexibility of her nakedness as if searching for a damning flaw. She had never considered herself voluptuous; she *wasn't* voluptuous with her small breasts, her girlish waist and hips. She slid her hands over the small, defined bones of her pelvis and shook her head at her fancy. Love: It made a woman conscious of what she was not, made her want to improve herself inside and out, to be vivacious with health, to be brilliant, the best, the only one.

After slipping her naked body into a pair of dark green slacks, she wriggled into a soft cream-colored cardigan sweater. She buttoned it on the way to brush her teeth and comb her hair. After applying a faint tint of lipstick, she searched for the door key. Telling Clifford the truth wouldn't take long, she reasoned. Perhaps then she could rest and not feel as if half of her were missing.

However, the decision which had seemed so clear-cut in her own room assumed different shades of foolishness once Victoria waited outside Clifford's door. The hallway was deserted. She glanced about herself as if she expected to find some sage piece of graffito which would advise her what to do. Why did a person, once they began to love someone, sprout an instant Achilles' heel?

She forced herself to tap softly on his door. Waiting, she rehearsed the optimistic things she would say when he opened it. The door made all the creaking, nervewracking, unlocking, opening sounds that were possible before it finally opened. At some point during the mechanics, every word she had been prepared to say woefully vanished from her mind. As he towered before her, naked to his waist, looking as if he had fought his way through the gates of hell, even her true purpose for coming evaporated. She gaped at the masterful stance of him and envisioned how utterly stupid she must look.

Distraught, she blurted, "Please don't be mad at me!"

Clifford folded his arms about her with a longing he felt only with her. She didn't see the easing of the deeply engraved lines down his face. He didn't kiss her; he only held her tenderly and she drew comfort from the throb of his heartbeat beneath her cheek. She wished he would say something reassuring, but he didn't. So, pressing the flat of her palms against the solidity of his back, she simply clung to him.

He kicked the door shut behind her. "What's the matter, love?"

He knew, even without explanations, what she had gone through, she thought gratefully. He wasn't going to look at her with one of those You-shouldn't-have-done-that expressions. She relished the feel of his large hands skimming the contours of her back to her waist. His pressure at the base of her spine drew her willingly closer to him, and his caress traced the symmetry of her back.

"I came to tell you I'm sorry." She wanted to say the words of apology now, even if they weren't necessary.

Clifford's chin balanced on the crown of her head as she spoke, and his fingers criss-crossed the width of her shoulder blades. She drew in her breath as he hesitated at the place where her bra should have transversed her back. During the seconds of his unhurried gesture, the casual smoothing of her hips, her logic whirled crazily. When one of his fingers slipped beneath the waist of her slacks and discovered the suggestion of her half-nakedness, she knew immediately what he assumed. She had made another mistake.

"You don't have to tell me that," Clifford was saying absently, his fingers tangling in her hair now.

"I do!" She guessed he wasn't even listening to her. "I mean, I don't believe that definition about love means never having to say you're sorry. Apologies need to be said, Clifford."

From the second Victoria's breasts had crushed against his chest—sensually free, provocative—Clifford's mind had spun off on an unchartered madness. Just knowing that she had come to his room wearing nothing but slacks and a sweater began a chain-reaction of daring in him. His need to make love to her nearly blinded him.

Placing his hands on each side of her face, he tipped it upward for long, shattering seconds. He doubted that she had any idea of what she had done. Thinking he should keep his hands off her, he took her shoulders and scrutinized her wide look of confusion.

"I probably shouldn't have come," she said lamely and began attempting to extricate herself from his hold. "I thought . . . I don't know what I thought, only that I felt like a wretch and I had to know you forgave me and . . ."

When he let her go without making a fuss, she gave him a brief, uncertain smile. He didn't step back from her, and she didn't move away. The danger of touching simply was there, and they both sensed it.

Presently Clifford wiped his hand down his jaw and said, "I would rather you were honest with me, Victoria."

Her naiveté was incredible, she thought wildly. She had, like a child, thought he would kiss her and tell her it was all right to accuse him of trying to buy her love. Maybe he would say he cared very much for her and send her on her way back to her room.

The corded muscles in Clifford's neck were not

perfect; they were rigid with tension and had turned a dull crimson. Unprepared to cope with such a blatant male arousal, she snatched her gaze away, as if it would politely erase his desire.

"I was being honest," she mumbled.

"You were toying with me."

"I was not!"

Her gaze darted back to him, but Clifford wasn't looking at her. His eyes watched his own hands as they reached for the fragile buttons on her sweater and methodically began undoing them.

"I didn't come for that!" she rasped and realized her resistance challenged him even more.

His hands impatiently gripped both sides of the sweater and deliberately yanked the garment apart. She was bare to the waist, and her hands involuntarily flew to mold about the thrust of her breasts.

Painlessly and effortlessly, he pulled her hands away and trapped them at her sides. "Why?" he demanded, and his voice was thick with urgency. "Why did you come to me in the middle of the night like this, knowing that I'm half crazy from wanting you. Do you think I have no limits to what I can stand? I can still smell the soap on you, Victoria," he muttered as his head bent swiftly. "You want what I want. Admit it."

The tip of his tongue touched her breast at its very center, circling the pinkness there. Speared by a sudden spell of drunkenness, Victoria didn't know if Clifford was right or not, or if she had the strength to stop him. Her needs might be as great as his, but her motives were not.

Her lashes dropped with silky exhaustion against her cheeks as her nipples reacted exactly as he intended them to. Her head dropped back to expose the ivory arch of her neck. "I told you," she moaned. "You know I can't."

"You can, and you will."

The arrogance of Clifford's certainty was as chilling as an icy blast on the back of her neck. Her whole body stiffened, and she instinctively pushed herself away from him. Her womanly dignity was only so much physical release to him! she thought crazily and knew instantly that it wasn't true. Yet she could not, would not tolerate being degraded. She struck at his determined hands and attempted to button her sweater.

"Don't, Clifford!" She refused to look at him.

Her abrupt aloofness stunned him. It curled the edges of his lips into a half-surly smirk. "Womankind never changes, does it?" He laughed cryptically. "Well, say no all you want to, I don't mind."

Her eyes glittered at the sarcasm in his tone. "Take your male ego and go back to bed, counselor. We'll talk when you're in a better frame of mind. I'm sorry I came."

Seeing her go was the last thing he wanted. Regretting his macho come-on, he lunged for her before she could reach the door.

In all of his life Clifford had never intentionally struck a woman. He had no intentions of doing so now. But as Victoria turned back to glimpse the swift movement of him reaching for her, she thrust out her arm. Clifford reacted with an automatic reflex. His hand glanced off her poised wrist with a painful clip which, considering the explosive tension between them, had the effect of shoving down the plunger on a detonator.

Dazed, not thinking clearly except that he had actually hit her, Victoria clenched both her fists and whirled toward him in a feral movement. Her confusion of only minutes before blazed into full anger. He had read her motives for coming much more accurately than she had, and that embarrassing realization enflamed her logic. She brought both her fists down on the exposed span of his chest in a reckless attack. She hit him hard more than once.

Swearing a surprised oath, Clifford threw up a forearm against her fiery outburst. Not wishing to hurt her, dodging what he could with raspy sounds of disbelief, he took one blow to his ribs which really hurt. Then he clamped his fingers about both her wrists with the bruising iron force he would use on a man.

"Stop it!" he ground out. *"I mean it, Victoria!"*

Victoria didn't care that the wreckage of the past day was rushing through the muscles of her own body. With all her female strength she battled John Carroll, the circumstances of Brayntree which had trapped her at their mercy, the love for a man she was powerless to express. She kicked at Clifford in a wild, blind pain until he twisted her arm and tripped her, sending them both tumbling to the floor.

Clifford could hardly hold her still and the feel of her breasts crushed hard against him, the twisting thrust of her body as she struggled to escape from beneath his vanquishing weight, pushed him past reason. Before he realized the frightful danger, he was kissing her. He ground his lips hard on hers, forcing his tongue into her mouth and fumbling between them for the zipper of her slacks.

"No!" she cried as she finally wrenched her mouth free of his bruising lips. "I'll never forgive you if you do!"

He only grinned down at her and pinioned her

from the waist up. "Oh, yes you
he promised her between his tee

When her fingernails clawed at
them, and she caught him off b
escape. Her slacks, when he grasp
over her hips and legs with a cutt
His rumbling sound of satisfaction
humiliation. She managed to crawl a few feet before
the breath was knocked from her as Clifford grasped
one ankle and jerked hard, sending her down again.

When he pulled himself up to straddle her back
she called him the most horrible names she could
think of. At the same time she was appalled at her
own breathtaking desire for him. When he wrestled
her sweater over the top of her head, the feel of his
urgent male need weakened her almost beyond her
ability to bear it. Never had she wanted anything as
badly as she ached for him! Unbelieving, morbidly
ashamed of her wantonness, she buried her face in
the bend of her arm so he couldn't see the drugged
glaze of passion clouding her eyes.

"You can't do this to me!" she groaned into her
arms as he flung her sweater aside.

"I am doing it." His voice grated harshly with
resolve.

Grasping both sides of her waist, Clifford dragged
her back to him until they fit like two perfect pieces
of the same puzzle. Only when the sweetness of her
hips conformed to his hard, manly angles did he
realize the enormity of what he was poised to do.

Slumping with disgust at his own lack of control
where this woman was concerned, Clifford shud-
dered at how close he had come to marring everything he had worked so diligently to build. The fire
of his intentions drained out of him like water

a sieve. He was left spent and bitter at
f. He felt like Cain.

At once he released her and numbly helped her
compose herself. Snatching a sheet from the bed, he
wrapped her gently in its snowy cocoon. He bent
forward and carefully cradled her in the protective
hollow of his body.

"Victoria," he choked out her name, "I didn't
mean to. I swear I'd never hurt you."

In the muted light of the room, a large space now
filled with the labored sounds of their own breathing, Victoria felt the distance yawning between
them. In an effort to hold onto the good things they
had, she huddled against his chest.

He smoothed back her hair in an automatic gesture of comfort. "It's all right. Everything's my
fault. I'm some kind of animal. I admit it. A cad, an
unmitigated degenerate, a lusting beast, a ravenous
wolf, a carnivorous vulture—"

Victoria smiled rather sadly. Draping her left arm
over his shoulder, she hushed him. "No, you're
not."

"I'm not?" His teasing was almost shy.

"You're not a carnivorous vulture."

He nuzzled her ear, and their tattered breathing
slowly subsided. "Tell me your heart, little one," he
said after a time. "I promise I'll listen this time."

Silence now would ruin everything. Victoria was
tired, but if they didn't talk tonight they might never
talk. She settled herself in the curve of his legs and
repeatedly smoothed at the sheet draping across her
knees.

"I don't think a person's background should be
held against them, Clifford."

"Neither do I. I don't hold yours against you.
What's to hold against?"

"I'm not as sexually free as a lot of women are these days."

Not knowing exactly what she was trying to tell him, Clifford agreed with her. What she said was true. "Free sex is very out of fashion now. Commitment is in."

She stiffened slightly in his arms. "Even if it weren't, I just can't tumble into bed for a one-night stand. Or even a two-night stand. I was raised to believe that when a woman loves a man she marries him."

Unaware that he had begun rubbing her spine with the tips of his fingers, he followed the line of her reasoning. "I never asked you for a one-night stand, Victoria. I told you from the beginning I loved you. And even though you didn't tell me then, I knew you loved me, too. The chemistry was undeniable, you know that. There's the problem with Faith, of course. But you know I'll work that out."

"I wish it were settled now."

She didn't say any more, and Clifford didn't dare turn her to face him for fear that the communication which had taken so long to reach would be broken. Giving her time, he delicately prodded her to continue.

"The wait won't hurt us. It'll make us better," he said.

"I don't argue with that. Only . . ."

"Only, what?"

"When a woman loves a man, she wants to know she comes first with him. She doesn't want to take second place to anything. No old sweetheart's feelings, not even a mother's."

He didn't reply at first.

"That's fair. When we get back home, I'll tell Mother and Dad. You can come with me if you want to, and we'll tell them together." He smiled with a sigh. "Does that make everything all right?"

Victoria ducked her head. When she didn't answer Clifford straightened his back, as if he feared the worst were upon him. "Honest to God, Victoria, I've done everything I know to do, promised you everything I know to promise. I took the money I was going to buy a house with and rescued your school from the pits."

Her protest bubbled in her throat, but he brushed her objection aside. "I don't want to haggle over that now. My point is, I've committed myself to you in every way I know. I love you madly, blindly. You're the only woman I've ever loved."

When Victoria leaned back in his arms to frown at his orderly logic, she was unaware that she had partially pulled herself from the modest tent of the sheet. To him, she looked like the splendid product of the hands of a Greek sculptor with only her shoulders covered. His eyes devoured the creamy hollow between her breasts, her navel, the tiny swell of her abdomen.

Yet she was so intent upon what she wanted to say, she didn't notice. Her lips opened several times, and her eyebrows carved a hesitant arch. She drew one quick breath, then let it out, telling him nothing.

"Say it!" he snapped at her. "Enough is enough."

A fool was nothing in comparison to what his irritation made her feel. Primitive pride choked off her words. Yet she knew with an old, old wisdom that this was not the time to be proud. Seeking the protection of his chest, she leaned her forehead on the hard expanse.

"You haven't asked me to marry you," she mumbled.

Clifford couldn't begin to comprehend the garbled

reply. Grasping her chin, he forced her head up. He stared at her until she couldn't outlast him. She lifted her dewy brown eyes.

"Now tell me again."

"I feel stupid saying it."

"Then feel stupid."

She was immeasurably stung by his lack of tact. This was nothing like the way a girl envisioned a conversation about marriage. But she tilted her chin regally. "You have never asked me to marry you," she repeated with exaggerated clarity.

For a moment, as his comprehension slowly dawned, Clifford didn't even try to express his surprise. He laughed. Giving his touseled head a shake, he held her at arm's length to make certain she was really serious.

"Is that *all?*" he choked.

She flushed. "Is that *all?* I'm still square enough to believe that it should be asked, and that the man should do the asking. Call me funny that way. In fact, I don't care what you call me. Let me up. I want to go back to my room."

"You're not going anywhere, my little goose," he assured her. "For heaven's sake, Victoria, you've known I wanted to marry you from the very beginning."

She smirked at him. "And how was I to know that? You wouldn't tell Faith about me. You wouldn't tell your parents. You wanted me to keep up the pretenses of your engagement."

He held up a contradictory finger. "I never wanted to keep my engagement. I swear, from the day I kissed you under that old gazebo I've not so much as touched Faith Chambers."

In spite of her wounded dignity, Victoria smiled a beautifully triumphant smile. Clifford laughed again.

"You jealous little imp! Now, tell me how special you think I am. My ego has just been ripped to shreds."

Her chin was firmly erect, and her smile gradually transformed into a frown. "You did it again, Clifford! Side-stepped it like it didn't even exist. I think you're doing it on purpose. I think I shouldn't believe a word you say."

"What did I do now?" he barked, brows knitted. "I'll declare."

"You—didn't—ask—me—again."

Pausing, his golden eyes slightly hooded with the thick furl of eyelashes, Clifford thought he had never loved her more than at this proudly petulant moment in her life. He wanted to kiss her hard and roughly. He wanted to bury himself against her and within her, never to be separated from her again. He forced himself to appear steady.

"Victoria Carroll," he said gravely, "will you marry me?"

Her shoulders sagged. "Now I've pushed you into saying it," she wailed softly. "It's not the same."

His fingers bit into her arms, and he gave her a loving shake. "Woman, are you going to say yes? Damn!"

Feeling that no matter what he did she would always be a step ahead of him, Clifford detached himself. The paces he took were halting, doubtful.

Victoria clutched the sheet, following him. She smiled at his back and knew he didn't understand. Her future had just emerged from the shadows. Knowing he would *be there* to share things with, to give daughters to, was like a miracle drug. It destroyed the clinging cobwebs of girlhood. In seconds it fashioned her into a woman. It made her bold and greedy. She went on her toes to kiss the back of his shoulder and felt his shiver. Her arms slipped silkily about his waist. "If you really want me," she said softly.

Clifford turned and filled his arms with her and the billowing sail of the sheet. Her lips moved pliantly beneath his now, more willing to be taken, reaching eagerly to venture.

"Want you?" he mumbled. "D'you want *me?* I'm only a man, Victoria. I make a lot of mistakes. I've made them with you."

"Shh." She placed her fingers on his lips. "You're what I want."

The play of her fingers tracing the ruff of his moustache made him incapable of moving. Their slender tips moved across his lips and touched his teeth. He felt the raw throb of desire and couldn't bring himself to ask it of her, not after what had happened before.

"Victoria—" he began.

"Hush," she said against his mouth. "Hush, now."

When she lifted her arms to twine about his neck the sheet slithered gracefully to the floor. Clifford was aware of the cloud of percale at his feet. He didn't kiss her but felt what she was telling him in the strain of her legs against his, in the urgency of her knees, in the palms of her hands which pulled his face nearer to hers. He knew she wanted him. He reached for the buckle of his belt.

"No."

He stopped immediately.

Her voice was rich with arousal. "Let me."

His pants were clumsy in her fingers, but she cast them aside without looking. She wasn't thinking of herself now, or her own skin glowing beautifully in the faintness of the light. She was absorbed in his magnificent strength. His sheer size and the hair on his legs which was the color of ripe wheat after a rain.

For lost seconds their eyes came together. They reached across the distance and knew that this time it was what they both wanted. It wasn't an accident. It was meant to be.

They found the kiss eagerly, like children. Her arms locked about his neck ferociously as his tongue met hers. He was amazed at the burn of her passion. Her mouth, escaping his, caressed the sinews running through his neck. Clifford let her follow her instincts and stood still. She seduced his fingers with dainty nibbling kisses until he reeled with a strange intoxication. As she ventured to his waist, he froze. Her touch was no longer part-girl, part-woman. Her hands spread possessively wide over the leanness of his hips, and as she bent, wraithlike and hesitant, moaning his name over and over, her arms folded about both his knees.

"I do love you, Clifford," she whispered and turned her face into the side of his thigh.

He didn't reply. He couldn't even breathe. Catching one of her hands, he drew it to the warm aching part of him which seemed, at that single heartbeat of time, to be the center of them both.

She closed her fingers about him perfectly.

Shaping his mouth about her name, unable to say it, Clifford let his eyes flutter closed. He filled his hands with the shimmery softness of her hair and then, with a sublime effort at self-control, slowly began to die.

Chapter Eleven

M y, my, Miss Victoria," Mamie Gardner beamed as she wiped her hands. She was gingerly trailing behind Victoria during the routine visit to Brayntree's kitchen. It was a week before Christmas. "A vacation was just what the doctor ordered. You're your old self again. So like your dear mother, if you don't mind me sayin' so, miss."

Victoria glanced up from writing on her clipboard. Smiling, she swept open the door to the flour pantry and peeped into the stainless steel bin. "Coming from you, Mamie, I consider that a compliment of the highest order."

"That's exactly what your mother would have done, too. Gone straight to that foreign place over there and set *that man* straight. Face to face."

Mamie never referred to John Carroll by his Christian name. The edges of Victoria's lips tightened at her misconception of just who had set whom straight in Austria. "I doubt that, Mamie," she said. "John got what he wanted, that was all."

Mamie refused to be swayed in her pride. Settling a turban back on her head, a garish length of orange chintz that made her look like a woman from the Louisiana backwater about to commence a voodoo ritual, she snorted and flicked her cleaning rag in disgust.

"You handled everything just right. *That man* only listens to money. It's all he ever listened to." Mamie's round face fell. Realizing her blunder, she said, "Beg your pardon, Miss Victoria. Sometimes I clear forget he's your father."

Victoria sighed and snapped the cap back on her pen. She clipped it inside the pocket of a flowing circular skirt which swirled beneath a fine but loosely woven pullover sweater.

"Don't worry. Sometimes I forget it myself. I must remind you, Mamie, just because we have Eliot off our backs, it's only a temporary respite. We'll have to economize more than ever now. What with Christmas, then the New Year's dance . . . well, I can hardly ask you to try harder." Her mouth twisted into a perturbed rosebud.

Mamie's pat to her forearm was her one gesture of affection. "Don't you worry, miss. I think you've worked a miracle as it is. We'll pay off the bank. You wait and see."

Victoria escaped the kitchen as quickly as she could. Her deception of Brayntree's staff regarding the school's financial situation was unintentional. With the exception of Stephanie, everyone automatically thought she had arranged financing at one of the banks. Once the error was made, it was much, much simpler to let them go on believing it. Being in partnership with Clifford Pennington was something she hadn't gotten used to herself. She had no idea in the world how to explain it to them.

Once she and Clifford had returned home from Austria, the first setback in their relationship proved to be the necessity of postponing telling Clifford's parents about their plans. Ethan Pennington, they discovered, had unexpectedly swept Madeline off to the Bahamas for a rest. They wouldn't return until just before Christmas.

"We'll tell them the minute they get back, darling," Clifford promised her on the telephone.

"Oh, I guess I'm really glad for the delay," she confessed to him. "I can't say I was looking forward to seeing the shock on their faces."

"They only want to see me happy, Victoria. Mother is getting much stronger. Just because Faith and I aren't marrying doesn't mean they can't be the best of friends."

"I would never intrude on something as special as that," she said and meant it heartily. She would simply have to believe in Clifford's judgment of telling Faith, wouldn't she? Silence, in this instance, was not only golden, it was the difference between trust and mistrust. A discrete tongue was needed now or she could ruin everything.

During the weeks after Thanksgiving the telephone provided the lifeline between Victoria and Clifford, which was a blessing since inhibitions tended to wander when one was snuggled beneath a warm blanket late at night and murmuring into a phone. He could be magically erotic, she learned, and she even ceased blushing at his suggestive intimacies. Loving him made her bold, and she parried his sensuality with her own. He adored it.

But conducting a courtship by telephone was highly unsatisfactory. She wanted desperately to see him, even for a few stolen moments. She didn't care how much of Ethan's workload Clifford had shouldered. She wrecked an entire afternoon's schedule so she could drive into Williamsburg.

"Hi, Devon," she said, smiling into the phone after rushing from a class in political science. "Could I speak to Clifford, please? I called his office and the secretary said he had come home early."

By now, Devon's shameless teasing was routine, practically expected. She guessed he knew most everything.

"Ahh," he said congenially, "I'm afraid she made a mistake, pretty girl. Cliff's out for the rest of the day. I'm afraid you'll have to settle for me. A real bargain, huh?"

Victoria felt a warning prickle electrify her nerves. "Oh, did Clifford say where he was going?"

"Lemme see, love, I think he said he was meeting Faith somewhere. Why? Something important come up?"

The sensation of having walked into a wrong room by mistake nearly strangled her. A whole ugly system of lies confronted her. How blind she had been! No, she argued, Clifford really loved her; she believed that. Then why hadn't he said, "It's necessary for me to see Faith. It's for us. It means nothing." Because he *couldn't* say that! She didn't know if she were big enough to accept this at face value.

She lied with appalling ease. "No, nothing's wrong. Clifford's handling some . . . ah, financial things for the school, as you probably know. I'm neck deep in planning the New Year's dance, that's all. I'm afraid it gets to be more of an unaffordable luxury every year."

Devon was so silent she guessed he didn't believe her. She was a bad actor with an even worse script.

"Oh?" he said at last.

She forced a laugh. "We always have the dance, though. It's so droopy after the new year when everyone comes back to school. We save our celebrating for the dreary times. Good thinking, huh?"

"Very good thinking."

"Yes, well, I guess I'll let you go, Devon. I hope I didn't interrupt anything."

"Wait!"

Victoria paused in the act of hanging up. Replacing the receiver to her ear, she tried to smooth the paranoid despair from between her brows.

"I'm pretty good at some things," he joked, not a trace of guile in his voice. "Planning New Year's dances is my forte. Why don't I fill in? I'm a great substitute for Cliff."

For a few moments she said nothing, only stood there nursing the tiny sting of anger that Clifford could put her in the position of finding out this way, like a wife discovering a husband's infidelity from a friend.

Finally she spoke. "Devon Pennington, what good thing did I ever do to deserve a friend like you? Where do you want to meet?"

He laughed. "Come by and pick me up. I've never ridden in a jeep before."

Victoria dressed in a frenzy. She snatched on a pair of black velvet knickers she had been saving to tease Clifford with and topped it with an ivory georgette blouse. After searching through her closet, she pulled out a soft leather battle jacket from several seasons back. That, plus her boots, put her in a reckless mood. Clifford was a free man! Which meant she was free, too. This was one evening she planned to thoroughly enjoy. She had to. She . . . just had to.

An evening with Devon Pennington was automatically entertaining. No matter how foul the mood, his courteous attentions were perfect medicine. He never let her forget what a desirable woman she was. He seemed to take great delight in driving her jeep, something she couldn't imagine Clifford doing. And he cracked jokes all the way downtown.

Ignoring her fleeting pangs of guilt that she was using him, Victoria returned his lighthearted flirtations. They browsed through shops until they closed. They planned the cost of a Roaring Twenties theme for the dance. Devon was supremely helpful, suggesting equipment she would need to build a mock bandstand and telling her where she could find pieces from antique cars to hang from the ceiling as decor.

Over pizza and wine at a small bistro near the college, talk dwindled to more serious subjects: Devon's career, the death of his older sister, and finally to Clifford and Faith.

"You're pretty hung up on Cliff, aren't you?" Devon did his probing in such a pleasant way she could hardly take offense.

She neatly avoided answering. "A girl's a fool if she gets hung up on a man, Devon."

"Fool," he smiled, "thy name is Victoria."

She glanced away, and he quickly covered her hand with one of his. "Look, Victoria, if you ever need anyone, let me know. I mean it."

Pain filled her eyes when she looked up at him. He

saw far too deeply inside her, but at least she didn't have to explain things. "Devon, please, I—"

"I think I'm a little in love with you myself."

Her smile was miserable. "Things are never simple. Or maybe it's me. Maybe I want too much, too fast. Do you mind terribly if we went home now?"

"Sure. But you remember what I said."

They were walking out the double doors when Victoria stepped directly into Clifford's path. The surprised expression on his face hardly registered on her; she wasn't interested in his face because his hands rested upon Faith's ribs, in that intimate around-the-waist looseness that she knew only too well. Over the wave of nausea which surged up into her throat, she stepped back against Devon's shoulder and slumped helplessly against the reassurance of his arm.

"Hello, Cliff," said Devon. "Faith, as always, you're ravishing."

Devon Pennington, Victoria thought dumbly, was a dying Southern breed! How could he be so perfect, so properly cordial, so heaven-sent?

Behind the granite mask of his face, Clifford could have been anything. If his chiseled jaw were any indication, he completely mistook what his glittering eyes saw as they swept over her. Unmoving, blocking the doorway, he nodded with a curt civility which was little less than insulting.

"Devon?" he murmured. His gaze levelled threateningly. "Victoria?" Not one trace of remorse tempered his anger.

Victoria was determined not to behave like an addled schoolgirl. She extended her hand to Faith with a numb remark of how nice it was to see her again. She disguised her wet, oozing fear of becoming caught up in a scene.

"I wish I could wear knickers," the blond woman said with a laugh. "I'm afraid they make me look like the scarecrow in the *Wizard of Oz*."

"I can't imagine anything doing that," Victoria returned politely.

The entire exchange, only a few seconds long, seemed to further infuriate Clifford. He moved forward with short, disturbed steps. Yet, due mostly to Devon's miraculous smoothness, the right partings were muttered, the correct amenities performed. Clifford and Faith proceeded in one direction while she and Devon went in the other.

Victoria forced herself to keep from turning around to watch the broad-shouldered offense Clifford bore as he walked away, nor his unfair, double-standard scorn. She wanted to cry, but instead she threw out her hand and stumbled against Devon as they walked across the dark parking lot toward the jeep.

"Oh!" she choked.

Dozens of smells assaulted her at once: rancid food cooking, rotting garbage cans in alleys, foul car exhaust, molding wet ground, even the stench of damp asphalt. She clamped her hand across her mouth in defiance of the pizza which threatened to come up as easily as it had gone down.

Taking her by the shoulders, Devon scoured over her pale, drawn features. "What's the matter?"

"I can't be sick!" she gasped and bent at her waist. "Not here!"

"Oh, yes you can, sweetie. Here, come with me."

Swiftly Devon steered her into the overgrown solitude between a row of box hedges and a deserted alley. Tossing him a final look of despair, Victoria leaned to her knees and unceremoniously lost her dinner.

It was some moments before she could talk again. Devon silently proffered her his handkerchief, and she blotted her lips, embarrassed to the roots of her hair. His arm was a godsend as they walked back to the jeep. She let him assist her into the seat and before he shut her in, he tipped up her chin with a thumb.

"Victoria, dear," he said with the gentlest voice she thought she had ever heard. "Are you pregnant?"

"No!" she blurted immediately. Then she stared past his head at the traffic blurring on the street beyond them. They all came back—the hours she and Clifford had spent making love. She shrank inwardly at her own private memories until she looked very small, very damaged. "I mean," she added with a bleak stare, "I don't know."

When Devon cleared his throat she came to herself and sought the invitation she knew would be in his eyes. "I really am a fool, after all, aren't I?" she said and let him slip beside her on the seat. With incredible tenderness he took her into his arms.

"Poor baby," he comforted. "My poor, poor baby."

That night Victoria went to bed with the telephone cradled beside her pillow. Surely, Clifford wouldn't be too angry to call. He *must* want to explain; she certainly did. And then there was the other. Oh, she would have to see a doctor, of course, but she knew the truth. She carried Clifford's baby. What would Helen Carroll think if she could see her now? A woman who depended upon her reputation to make her living must be correct. Correct? Oh, God, *correct*?

For hours she lay staring through the half-darkness at the telephone. Clifford had totally misinterpreted why she and Devon were together. Was it possible she was misjudging him? Could she have misread that familiar intimacy which reeked from the two of them? Was he waiting beside his phone for her to call him?

Propping herself up on an elbow, Victoria dialed Clifford's number. Panicking, she slammed down the receiver and felt her heart pounding as if it would burst. She couldn't call first. She was right this time. She just couldn't go first.

Her telephone never rang.

"Miss Carroll!" Doris Everman shrieked from the second story window of the classroom overlooking the front lawns of Brayntree. "We're being invaded!"

"Invaded?" a dozen voices echoed in response.

After that particular cataclysmic statement, what power on earth could have prevented a mass of feminine faces from pressing against the windows which sparkled in the brilliant January sunshine? They had been practicing the finer aspects of grooming, makeup and hair styling, and at least half the class's heads were wrapped in towels fashioned like turbans. They looked, Victoria thought, like bobbing rows of early spring tulips as they all strained to look outside.

"What does the sign on the van say, Sennica? You've got good eyes," said Doris.

On tiptoe, peering over Dina's shoulder, Sennica squinted at an antiquated van making its way up the curved driveway toward the school. Since Victoria moved more slowly these mornings, a rather efficient way to avoid the queasiness of nausea, she tried unsuccessfully to glimpse a view between Betty and Roberta.

"I can't read it," Sennica reported, "but the pickup truck says 'Custom Remodeling. Harry Remmer, General contractor.' What d'you suppose they want?"

"Maybe they've got the wrong place."

"Jack let 'em in the gate, dummy," Doris reminded with condescending practicality. "Is it something for the dance, Miss Carroll?"

Victoria had no idea what it was for, but she had no doubts as to its source. Clifford Pennington: the father of her child, the man she had been trying unsuccessfully to break the news to for weeks. The fracture which had ruptured between them hadn't healed. It had grown worse. Now the days held such empty courtesies, such strained pleasantries, the words *I'm pregnant* simply refused to come.

She craved to make demands of him. She wanted to know everything. Why had he been with Faith Chambers that night? Why didn't they ever talk of marriage anymore? Was it over between them?

Clifford, however, offered no explanations, and Victoria pretended her anguish wasn't there. She behaved as if the constriction of silence were not destroying her, and she stubbornly kept her secret.

"Everything for the dance is arranged, Doris," Victoria said too abruptly. "This is some business which I must tend to. I'll send Stephanie up right away. You girls might as well put yourselves back together."

"Look!" Dina's throaty Garbo voice demanded their attention. "It's that *adorable* Porsche. Oh, it's Mr. Pennington! Betty, get these rollers out of my hair."

"Get them out yourself. I have only one eyebrow plucked. No one can see me like this!"

At the mention of the Porsche Victoria's lips

compressed. He was here. Maybe this would be the day. Maybe today she could tell him about the baby. "Stephanie will be right up," she snapped. "Get this mess cleaned up."

"Gravy!" Doris exclaimed as they all watched her stride out the door, grim-shouldered and determined. "What did we do?"

"Who cares?" Sennica groaned from the window. "Oooo, why doesn't she marry that gorgeous thing? Then we could see him every day. Just think—in the dining room, in the gym. Can you imagine what that hunk looks like in a pair of shorts?"

"Is that all you think about, Sennica? Men?"

Sennica's eyebrows arched in a spoiled-rotten haughtiness. "Darling, besides soap operas, is there anything else?"

Victoria tried to remain calm as she walked down the stairs, but she found her feet skimming, running down the steps, hurrying along the corridor. When she stepped into the cold brightness outside, hundreds of tiny flutters rippled along her nerves. Her eyes swept the drive, searching for the sight of him which would assuage the hunger gnawing through her limbs.

Clifford was unfolding himself from the Porsche. He ducked his head with the unconscious grace of a tall man. Standing, he appeared taller and more remote than ever as he shaded his eyes and squinted at the sun, then at the stable. His jeans beneath the fleece-lined jacket were faded. His western boots were scarred. An old knit cap perched rakishly on the back of his head, as if he willed himself to be cheerful.

She walked up behind him, certain of herself. "What do you think you're doing?" she asked, not meaning for the words to come out so abruptly.

He looked, not at her, but at the pickup backing toward the doors of the stable. "A little more, John. Back . . . back . . . there." His palm turned outward. "Hold it."

Peering into the truckbed, she saw it filled with sawhorses, droplights, extension cords and all kinds of power tools. The driver threw open his door, and two eager-faced college students climbed out, their arms bulging with rolled blueprints and plans.

Her certainty vanished. "Now wait just one minute," she began. She pointed a warning finger at the two students.

But Clifford, signaling his men with his brows, jabbed a thumb toward the stable and grinned down at Victoria's scowl. The men proceeded with their unloading, and Victoria braced both her fists on her hips.

"If it's not asking too much of you," she said tightly, "I'd like to know what's going on here, Pennington."

He drawled out his answer. "I'm protecting my interests, sweetheart. What are you doing?"

With a sinking realization she knew she couldn't tell him about the baby. Not today. Not in this mood. She flinched a little as his eyes made a rather prolonged scrutiny of her bulky tangerine sweater and the lines of her gray slacks. As he casually took one of her arms and began drawing her several steps beyond the working men, she snatched her arm free. She didn't want him touching her; it only made the hurt seem worse.

"I'm protecting my interests, too, Clifford. This is my property. You're trespassing."

His teeth glittered beneath the moustache. "Uh-uh. Only half trespassing. Half this place is mine. I'm putting an office on my part." He gestured with a jut of his jaw. "John, put that table saw on the right, just inside the door."

It was, naturally, his outlandish manner that triggered her temper, not the office. She thought he probably did it on purpose, as if the truth between them were too dangerous, a precipice projecting over the most deadly of rocks. She shivered violently.

"Cold?" he asked with unexpected gentleness.

He shrugged out of his jacket and draped it about her shoulders before she could object. He walked her, pushed her actually, toward the rundown building which housed the well-fed Daisy and two other horses. Victoria could imagine, as she snuggled into the warmth of the jacket, that every pair of eyes in the school must surely be glued to them. She could just hear what Sennica was saying at this very moment: *"Look, Doris, she's wearing his jacket. How divine!"*

As he prodded her past the open doors he leaned over the top of her head. "Wanna make love?" he murmured.

Before that night with Faith she would have flung herself at him. Now she stopped in her tracks and defied his intimacy with a glance which should have, by all rights, withered him on the spot. "I'm afraid, Clifford Pennington, there are others in front of me for that esteemed privilege. The line forms to the rear."

Her reaction was not what he had hoped for. His hands, when they fell on her shoulders, were too heavy with determination. Even through his jacket his fingers bit into her arms.

"Look, my bristly little porcupine," he ground out, "I've taken the lash of your tongue for weeks now. I'm damn well getting fed up with it."

She brushed back a lock of her hair. Her hand shook so badly she jerked it to her side. He hadn't denied a thing. She had accused him outright of making love to Faith and he had said nothing! They had slept together!

"Then pack up your toys and go play in someone else's sandbox, Clifford," she said, hating the truth which was beginning to sicken her. "How do you think—"

"I think," he lashed out, "that you have blown this whole thing out of proportion. And while we're on this subject, my love, I could say a few things about you and Devon. Do you—"

"Devon has nothing to do with—"

"Like hell he—"

"Will you let me finish?" She practically shouted at him.

The college boys, stopping suddenly, shot furtive glances toward the shadowy area where Victoria and Clifford stood glaring at each other. Taking her arm, Clifford drew her further behind the stacked crates. With an odd, sinking feeling, she recalled when she and Stephanie exchanged confidences sitting on these very crates. A lifetime ago another person, a very young girl, had told her friend how much she loved Clifford and that she feared that love would end up killing her. How remarkably accurate her predictions had been!

"No, I will not let you finish," he was saying. He pinned her back against the wall with his body. The muscular force of his limbs seemed packed with the pent-up frustration of weeks, and now it strained against hers, having nothing whatsoever to do with love.

Victoria had no warning of the kiss when Clifford suddenly dipped his head and took it. There was a depth of defiance in the moving of his lips on hers that shocked her. She hated it. She wanted to strike at him, to keep her lips tightly shut against him. She carried his child and he couldn't give her all of himself, not even now as his lips came down hard on hers.

His tongue darted into her mouth with a short-lived pleasure. This was all wrong, an act of force like the slapping of a face. *I will hurt you back,* she thought. Instead of resisting him she shut her mind and rejected him. He felt the rejection at once and released her: flushed, angry, mocking.

Her words were completely toneless. "I expect you let Faith finish."

His intake of breath was harsh. "Oh, yes," he said with tightly harnessed fury, "you can really twist the knife, can't you? Perhaps if you'd just once cared enough to trust me, we wouldn't be going through this now. And while we're on the subject of finishing things, leave Devon alone, Victoria. I don't like having the urge to strangle my own brother."

"How dare you say that? I told you Devon had—"

"And I told Faith!"

She knew exactly what he meant, and the impact of his confession took her fight away. How long had he waited to finally tell Faith? And would he ever have told her, the mother of his child? Was he punishing her for some unknown sin, letting her dangle, wondering about it? How very, very cruel.

"I suppose she was hurt," she said, for she had to say something to cover her own pain.

"Yes. She'll get over it."

It was unforgivable. Victoria turned and slowly walked away.

"Victoria!"

Victoria didn't answer him. This was one of those

horribly infectious things which, if not talked out, grew into a malignancy. But she was too wounded to talk, even though she wanted nothing but his healing arms about her, his body holding her.

By the doorway, where the darkness surrendered to the light outside, she paused with the resignation of someone who has lived a long time. She carefully removed his jacket and, with a look which Clifford thought was bottomless with hurt, she draped it on a peg beside the door. As if she were saying in her unemotional way, *Now it is over*.

He didn't go after her, though he could have. He stood there cursing his silent impotence and despising the misery which stretched before him for all eternity. He had wanted her to trust him without explanations. He should have told her; it wouldn't have lessened him. Being at one's weakest, when one is in love, is the time of greatest strength. Had he learned that too late?

His forehead dropped forward to make a cracking sound on the aging frame of the door. A pain shot through his head. He didn't care. He wished it had gone through his damnable heart.

Chapter Twelve

Stephanie, dressed in her best long gown, drew her knees up beneath her chin and wrapped her arms about her legs. "You're asking too much, Victoria," she advised futilely. Victoria sat with crossed legs in her chair before the fireplace in her room, sipping hot tea to settle her stomach.

Upstairs, in happy confusion, the girls were finishing their dressing for the gala occasion. The parents who were attending were arriving in a constant stream of strange and varied automobiles. Dates from town kept the telephones tied up with last-minute emergencies. In the kitchen Mamie and two extra hired girls were going quietly mad. Heaven only knew what Jack and Bud and the maintenance men were doing.

It was like this every year with the dining hall miraculously transformed into a ballroom. Somehow, in the end, it all meshed together for a grand success. This year would be no different, Victoria supposed.

"Besides," the assistant teacher went on and took the last puff from her cigarette as she talked. "You really have no choice except to marry Clifford. Not if you want to keep your reputation and continue operating this school. Having a baby as a single parent is one thing I don't think your parents would tolerate, no matter how devoted they are to you."

Victoria smiled and smoothed the textured folds of her mauve georgette evening gown. The metallic silhouette of her slingback high heels peeped from beneath its frothing yards of hem. She gently rocked her foot up and down. She dreaded this night beyond measure.

"There's no question about getting married, Steph," she sighed. "That was settled a long time ago. At least Clifford will be good to me. I'll make him a good wife. It's just that . . ." Sighing again, she replaced her cup to the tray. "For a while I thought we had something different. That once-in-a-lifetime love, you know. I was so sure."

Stephanie shook her head. She hated seeing Victoria blame herself for something she accredited to Clifford Pennington entirely. She hadn't forgotten warning him that night he came looking for Victoria. "You have to tell Clifford about this baby, Victoria. You can't wait another day."

"He's coming tonight." Victoria's apprehension welled up. "He said he was bringing his parents to see the school. Isn't that a laugh?"

"We-ell," Stephanie growled deep in her throat, "I doubt it's the school they want to see."

"Perhaps," Victoria mused, not listening to the other woman, "perhaps if we'd held out until we got married to . . . have sex. Oh, God, that sounds so cold. *Have sex,* like it was driving a car or unlocking a door."

"Now you're being too hard on yourself. I doubt that it was all that raw."

With a mannerism of one who is at the mercy of fate, Victoria dropped her face down to her fingers. "They say this is a liberated age we live in. Don't you believe it."

Stephanie's sniff was unapologetically disillusioned. She no longer believed in dreams of romance. "You two have liberated yourselves right into a corner with all this talk about the great, one-time passion. The man will marry you, Victoria. Take it from one who's been there. Grab what you have and be grateful. You could be having to marry a man who despises you."

But Stephanie couldn't understand what had been at the tips of her fingers, Victoria mourned to herself. Rising, she smoothed the pewter metallic belt tied about her slightly thickened waist.

"We have to get out there with all those giggling girls, my dear friend. Once again the Christians are condemned to walk amongst the lions."

Laughing, Stephanie suddenly stepped forward to gather Victoria into her arms. "Oh, Victoria, everything will be all right. You're one of the strongest young women I've ever known. If you and Clifford don't have a perfect beginning, you'll grow into it. I'm sure of that. In his way he cares very much for you."

Victoria hugged Stephanie in return. "You're a good friend. I wish I could repay you."

"You have. A dozen ways you don't even know."

Embarrassed by so much display of affection, Stephanie detached herself and sniffed loudly. She moved to the door of Victoria's bedroom and held it open with the teasing flourish of a musketeer. Bowing low, she murmured, "Pregnant ladies before sensible ones, mademoiselle."

"You're just jealous," Victoria said, smiling as she bravely approached the lions.

The rich smell of fresh-baked pastry and candlewax perfumed the entire lower floor of the house. It was a fragrance she always associated with Helen Carroll. Music blended festively with the gaiety of happy voices. The air tingled with excitement.

Victoria didn't worry about the mechanics of hospitality when Mamie was in charge of a party. Mamie had been trained by one of the great hostesses of all time. The ballroom would be decorated to expert perfection. The lighting would be subtle enough to hide the fact that the room was still a dining hall. Selected parents would eagerly perform as chaperones, lifting that duty from Victoria's shoulders. Victoria's only responsibility would be to circulate and be her sparkling best.

"Miss Carroll," Doris hissed in exaggerated secrecy as she sidled up beside her. *"Please* have a Paul Jones tonight. I'm just *dying* to ask Mr. Pennington to dance. D'you think he would?"

Victoria assumed her most effective pretense at shock. "Good heavens, Doris, your guess is as good as mine."

Doris puckered her mouth deliciously as her date, one of the local boys who would never have a chance to play second fiddle to the college professor, discovered her. "Well, find out, will you?" Doris whispered over her shoulder. "And let me know. I wouldn't want to make a fool of myself."

Victoria forced down a smile. "I wouldn't dream of letting that happen, Doris," she replied as her prime troublemaker whirled off on the arm of the unsuspecting young man. She lifted a tulip glass of punch from one of the long white-clothed tables running the length of the room.

"What does that girl want now?" Stephanie inquired, joining her.

Giggling, Victoria said, "Would you believe she wants me to fix her up with Clifford? Oh, the undaunted courage of the young."

"Speaking of courage, I think your intended just walked out to the stable with his parents. Showing off his new project, undoubtedly. My suggestion is that you get the ordeal over with in private and then enjoy the rest of the evening by dancing with every man here."

"Enjoy?" Victoria lifted her glass to the teacher in a doubtful salute. "There'd have to be something a lot stronger in this glass for me to enjoy this evening."

Glancing about the ballroom, smiling contentedly at the scene of her girls going through their social graces—something they all took very seriously in their preparation for being polished housewives, business executives, hostesses for future politicians and well-poised women in general—Victoria nodded. She replaced her glass on a tray for the empties.

"You're right, of course. I won't have a minute's peace until this thing is over with." She grasped Stephanie's fingers and crushed them. "Wish me luck, Steph. This could be the beginning of something very special or the ruination of me."

"Think positive."

"It isn't in me."

"Well, smile through your negativism, then."

Pasting an utterly ridiculous smile on her face, Victoria made her way across the crowded floor to search for a shawl she always kept hanging in the pantry beside the rear entrance of the house. She knew perfectly well why Clifford had invited his parents to this party. And it wasn't to see the school. She felt a very proper, and very irreversible, despair.

By the time Victoria stepped out into the January darkness, dew beaded on the ground and the evergreen shrubs. Caught in the moonlight, the lawns and the bordering bay in the distance shimmered beneath a diamond-studded canopy. From somewhere far away the melancholia of a boat's horn added its musical orchestration.

Victoria truly wished Clifford hadn't brought his parents out to the most neglected part of the property first. Having them receive a good impression of the school was important to her. Her breath came quickly as she hurried to welcome Clifford's parents to Brayntree and take them back into its warm hospitality.

A twig, catching the fringe of her shawl in its thorny fingers, tugged at her, making her pause. She bent to free it and as she straightened a lone pair of headlights raked across the gaunt stone of the mainhouse. Since dozens of cars were already parked in the driveway she dismissed it as a latecomer. Turning back, she continued her trek across the lawn to the stable.

"Victoria?" called a familiar voice.

She shaded her eyes and squinted back at the blinding lights. "Devon?"

Immediately Devon doused the lights. The car door slammed, and his slender shadow flitted swiftly across the driveway until she could see him clearly in the security lights. Hugging herself, she waited for him.

He laughed as he stepped near her. "Looks like a great party you got goin' here," he drawled.

Frowning, Victoria noted the rumpled furls of hair tumbling over his forehead and the tie drooping beneath his unbuttoned collar. She wasn't certain if she should scold him or smile; he was unmistakably tipsy.

"I think you've already had your own party, Devon," she chastised him gently.

Devon gave her a sheepish shrug and began peeling the wrapper off a piece of chewing gum. Folding it into his mouth, he apologized. "Sorry about that, pretty lady. I was taken by a slight seizure of the doldrums." He grinned down at her with a crooked boyishness.

Victoria winced at the bourbon on his breath. "I think the seizure was more than slight. You know your parents are here, don't you?"

"Really?" His sandy brows lifted, then puckered. "Yeah, I knew they would be. Cliff too, the rat. Thought I'd drive out and crash the party. You don't mind, do you?"

She let Devon fold her arm comfortably through his, or perhaps it was the other way around. His steps were none too steady as they matched hers. "You could never crash one of my parties," she fondly disagreed. "Why didn't you call me, Devon? I recall having a few seizures of the doldrums myself. The blind could have led the blind."

Chuckling contentedly, Devon removed his arm to wrap it securely about her shoulders. His uncustomary lack of prudence made Victoria uneasy as they weaved through the messy rubble of remodeling. Old lumber was piled about, and the new was neatly stacked. A couple of ladders leaned against the outer wall.

"Oops! Not that way, love," he laughed and drew Victoria firmly against the front of his legs. He raked over her concerned features. "Don't you know it's bad luck to walk underneath a ladder?"

He had her pinned so intimately to his length she could hardly breathe. One of his arms moved alarmingly across her back and the other large hand slipped up to cradle the back of her head. She knew only too well he wanted her—not only her friendship and her comfort, but a different kind of love than she was capable of giving him. His sweetness broke her heart.

"Devon—" She pushed against his chest a bit, not sure if he would let her go or not.

His fair head bent low over hers. "Victoria," he said brokenly, "I'm leaving tomorrow to go overseas, a dig that's been planned for months. I couldn't leave without seeing you, saying goodbye."

Tipping up her face, she studied the hopeless yearning which burned in his reddened eyes. He was so uncomplicated in his love for her that she wanted to hold him against her breast and rock him back and forth like a hurt little boy. "Ah, Devon," she said and cut through the pretenses as they had always done. "Things are never fair, are they?"

Freeing one of her hands, she cupped it tenderly about the curve of his jaw. Devon, even in his inebriated state, knew the truth. But he had drunk just enough to lose control over his good judgment. He turned his mouth into the softness of her palm and kissed it. His manly demands pressed him harder than he could bear, and he was suddenly holding her against passions which soared. His lips brushed eagerly across the dewy curve of her forehead, over the slope of her cheek to the delicacy of her ear.

"I know you don't love me," he said hoarsely, "not like a woman loves her lover. But I'd marry you, you know. I'd be a terrific father to this baby, and Cliff would never have to know."

"Devon!" The situation had grown deadly. Victoria began pushing from him in earnest, but he held her too tightly.

"Don't marry Clifford," he begged against her jaw. His breath fell warm and pleading. His hands urgently caressed her back. "Come with me. We'd have a good life together. I promise you. I swear t'you."

Victoria's face was buried in Devon's chest. She never heard the soft footsteps behind them, only the harsh intake of breath before Clifford spoke.

"I suggest you let her go, Devon," he said with a control more dangerous than Victoria had ever heard.

Freezing with horror, not aware that her own eyes were pressed shut, Victoria expected Devon to release her and step away. He didn't. He drew her around in the curve of his arm and drew his body quite tall beside her. She guessed he was nearly sober now, and she was forced to lift her own head to view the stark fury she knew would stain Clifford's face.

In the doorway beyond Clifford, clinging to the shadows, she barely glimpsed Madeline Pennington emerging on the arm of her husband. If ever Victoria wished she could die this was the time.

"What did you say?" Devon asked quietly, all frivolity gone now. "Oh, hello, Mother. I was looking for you."

Madeline, with her astute woman's eye, swiftly assessed the situation. Her eyes passed over Victoria with a surprising lack of blame, without any emotion, Victoria guessed, unless it was unadulterated pity. She spoke. "Devon, you've been drinking."

Devon's lips curved downward at one side. "Yeah. And done some things, said some things. Sorry, Clifford, old man. Dad—"

"I *said*," Clifford interrupted as he took an ominous step closer, "to let her go."

By now Victoria was shaking so badly she could hardly grasp the repercussions which followed in unexpected succession. She knew Ethan Pennington had positioned himself near Devon's right side, but her ears still rang with the threat lurking in Clifford's voice. She attempted, once, to pry herself free from Devon's persistent grip.

"Why?" Devon recklessly challenged his brother. "So you can make her cry again? Hmm?"

The muscle in Clifford's jaw twitched with rage. Suddenly, without warning, a smile blinked beneath the brush of his moustache. His words were half-teasing, urging. "Victoria doesn't need this, Devon," he said. "Come on, let me walk you back to your car. Better still, you'd better let Dad drive you home."

Devon wasn't too drunk to be slapped by the patronizing tone in his older brother's voice. He had watched Clifford win too often in the early years. Now it all came hurtling down upon him in a huge craving to get even.

"How would you know what she needs, Clifford?" he snarled defensively. "It's me she comes to. It's my shoulder she cries on. It's me she tells she's pregnant."

Madeline's soft gasp snapped Victoria's eyes wide open, just in time to keep her from stumbling when Devon abruptly released her. The whole world seemed to explode in a holocaust beyond anyone's ability to control. Clifford's steps were hardly visible. But his fist, when it clipped Devon neatly beside the nose, made a dull, crunching impact.

Victoria choked a small cry, but it was too late to keep Devon's head from snapping backward. His knees bent, and then he stumbled forward, one hand outstretched in an instinctive lunge to keep himself from falling. Ethan caught the shoulder of his youngest son and turned, in one outraged movement, to face his older one.

"I didn't raise a couple of savages, Clifford! Come to your senses!"

His words were not needed. Clifford had already realized the magnitude of what he had just done. Even the words which had triggered the violence were temporarily forgotten as Devon drew all their attention. He fished in his pocket for a handkerchief and held it to his bleeding nose. The silk, immediately soaked, was refolded, and Ethan dismissed Clifford's twisted remorse to find another handkerchief.

"Ohh," Devon groaned from behind his hand.

Madeline's strength seemed to arise in the emergency. Victoria stood speechless, shivering, unable to keep her teeth from chattering as Clifford ruefully rubbed his knuckles.

"Ethan," Madeline said in a cool, authoritative tone, "take Devon home before he attracts the attention of Victoria's guests. I'll drive myself home."

For too many years Ethan and Madeline had shared the rigors of child-raising to quibble about such a trivial thing as Madeline's ability to drive herself home. He and Devon disappeared into the shadows like the eerie fadeout on a movie screen.

"And *you*, Clifford," the imperious woman continued, "I'm taking this child inside. Keep yourself out of my sight for a few minutes before I do the same to you as you have done to your brother. On second thought, see if you have the discretion to find something to drink in the house. Come, Victoria. I've no doubts that my clever son can find us."

The arm which slipped about Victoria's shoulders was comforting, reassuring and completely trustworthy. She leaned against it with more sagging relief than she had felt for a long time. In Madeline Pennington she had an unexpected ally. She wanted to weep her gratitude.

"Where can I take you so we won't bring down the house with curiosity?" the woman inquired soon to be her mother-in-law.

"This way," Victoria choked, "to my rooms."

They walked to the side entrance, their steps in unison: two women in a crisis, depending on the unspoken but certain strength of the other. Neither of them looked back to see if Clifford were finding his way or not.

Clifford felt no slight; he hardly noticed them. He was much too confounded by the realization of his impending fatherhood.

Madeline's glance about Victoria's room was superficial; she was concerned about the state of the withdrawn young woman who moved to seat herself before the dressing table. Without asking where anything was, Madeline stepped to remove Victoria's shawl and place it upon the bed. Walking to the bathroom, she ran a glass of water and returned to place it on the table.

Victoria sipped, wondering as she did so what would happen next. How much did Clifford's mother know? Except that in her own body lay the first Pennington grandchild? A deep intensity clung to Madeline, and Victoria didn't know her well enough to guess if it warned of good things or bad.

From behind her, Madeline lifted her head. They gazed at the reflections of the other in the mirror. They started to speak at the same time, smiled, then waited.

Madeline went first. "I want to tell you from the outset, Victoria, that I'm sorry for the way I behaved when we met. I was coming out of a very difficult period of my life. That, of course, is no excuse, but—"

Nervous, needing something to do, Victoria began brushing her hair. "There is very little you can explain to me about grief, Mrs. Pennington. I have grieved. I still grieve."

"Over Faith? You shouldn't."

"I never meant to intrude into anyone's life. Clifford and I have hurt Faith, and that must bring pain to you, too. I'm sorry."

With a straightforward gesture, Madeline lifted the brush from Victoria's hand and arranged the waves capping the back of Victoria's head. For a moment neither of them spoke, as the knowledge of their touching welded its invisible foundation.

"When you've lived as long as I have, dear," Madeline finally explained, "you learn to know human nature. Only when a woman loves a man with deep passion can she be destroyed by him. I've always known that such a passion was never between Clifford and Faith. But I was so wrapped up in my own grief for Lisa, I let it go. That was my mistake."

"Not a mistake," Victoria disagreed, turning to peer up at the older woman.

Madeline shook her head. "Yes, a mistake.

Clifford did what he did because he loved me, not Faith. Faith will be fine."

Choosing her next words cautiously, Victoria said, "Mrs. Pennington, Clifford has asked me to marry him. Did he tell you that?"

When Madeline replaced the hairbrush on the table Victoria watched the elegant movement of her hands. The woman's steps were tired now, but still poised. "No," she replied. "But his father and I would have insisted. I don't have to be drawn pictures. Clifford's been a bear. I guessed before now he was falling in love with you."

The sting of satisfaction pricked deep inside Victoria. She needed to move about. Never in her talks with her own mother had she felt so emptied of herself. The relationships established in this room, this moment, would affect three lives. How she wanted Madeline to accept her and come to love her!

Her eyes fell to the floor, and she smoothed a ruff in the carpet with the toe of her sling. "I risk a good deal to speak to you of this," she said honestly. "It's difficult to risk loving a man as I do Clifford . . . with everything. But now, with you . . ." She felt at a loss. "If you, I mean, I could never hope to take Lisa's place. No one could do that. And Faith is such a dear, dear friend. But if you—"

Victoria lifted her pleading eyes. She didn't know how to say that she wanted to help fill the terrible void in Madeline's life.

The tap at the door was light but insistent. Without thinking about anything except the hurt that Madeline was capable of inflicting on her, Victoria opened it. An adorably chagrinned Clifford slouched in the opening. He rubbed his moustache.

"Clifford," his mother exclaimed in a tone which

made Victoria smother a smile, "if you have the nerve to show your face after that performance, come in."

Even Madeline's chastisement of her grown son, however, couldn't disguise the deep love she had for him. Clifford sent her a wry smile and stepped into the room. He kicked the door shut and in the same movement he took Victoria by the shoulders.

"Are you all right?" he murmured possessively.

"Are *you* all right?"

He grinned bleakly. "I asked you first."

"Clifford!" Victoria warned, exasperated.

From the corner of her vision, Victoria glimpsed the first awkwardness she had seen in Madeline tonight. Clifford seemed oblivious. With concern cutting his forehead, he drew Victoria into his arms and fit her chin into the web of his hand.

"Devon was telling the truth, wasn't he?" The question came gently, the golden eyes probing so intently Victoria flushed. "You're carrying . . ." he sighed, "part of us."

"I've tried to tell you for weeks, Clifford. I . . . well, things just kept growing from bad to worse, and—"

"That's not your fault," he said quickly.

"Yes it is. I behaved like a child."

"I knew you'd jump to the wrong conclusion," he insisted, "and it made me so damned mad."

Her lower lip began to tremble. She bit it hard. "I can't bear it when you're mad," she whispered thickly. She forgot Madeline as she coped with the urgency of Clifford's tightened embrace.

Madeline's gown rustled as they held each other, and the unobtrusive movement snapped Victoria back to her senses.

"Clifford," Madeline stepped forward, "I pride myself on being a sophisticated woman. But not this sophisticated. I will leave you two to settle this between you. Only, please, accept my heartfelt blessing on whatever you do."

The marked silence as the two women looked at each other needed no words of explanation. Victoria knew beyond any doubt that Madeline was giving her an answer to the question. The exquisite silver head bent as she placed a kiss on Victoria's cheek. Almost immediately she straightened and smiled. Quietly, a bit hoarsely, she said, "Life is very short, Victoria. Please be happy. Know that you are loved."

With a weighty sense of gratitude, perhaps humility too, Victoria watched Madeline walk bravely to the door and let herself out.

"It's so sad," she choked to the shut door. "She's not over it yet."

Beside her Clifford felt like a mountain. His eyes pierced somewhere where she couldn't follow, nor did she want to. He was in the past, and the past held little that was good for her.

Turning suddenly, he smiled down at her. "She'll be all right. She and Faith'll still be good friends. Then, there's you." Grinning, he slipped a large hand to her waist. "And . . . that. Where Mother only had one to love, now she'll have two. That will make her happy, you'll see."

Without warning the old fear was there, the nagging dread of losing that which was not quite won. "And will we two make you happy, Clifford?"

"What d'you mean, happy? Of course I'll be happy."

As she detached herself from him, walking several

steps beyond and half-muttering to herself, she could feel his eyes drilling into her back. "There're better ways to arrange these events, you know," she said.

With the safety of distance between them, she turned, sending the swirls of her skirt billowing about her feet. "Even though everything has been said," she blurted emotionally, "I could make it on my own, Clifford. You don't have to marry me."

He was across the room in three turbulent strides. There was no self-protection about his brows, no egotism in the compulsion of his step. His lips thinned into a line of offense that she should throw the choice at him in this way.

The jacket to his suit fell open as he twisted, a sinewy structure of pure male determination. A powerful arm shot out for her, and he crushed her against his chest. Any protests she tried to utter were smothered with impetuous, fiery kisses. When his moustache scraped her face, she didn't care. He was pressing the breath from her, and she didn't even close her eyes, lest she miss the welcome sight of him needing her this badly.

"You'll hear me this time," he muttered thickly as he caught a ragged breath. "I'll say it loud and clear."

"What?" She was dizzy from his hands filling themselves with her hips, lifting her, grinding her against him.

"That I die a little when I'm not with you. Nothing matters without you. Nothing. And it's not the baby. It's you. *You, dammit!*"

Her head snapped backward as he picked her up. She felt her skirt tangling between his legs as he carried her. Behind them was a sofa and he turned toward it. They tumbled on it in a whispering froth of skirt, and she groaned his name over and over until he covered her with his weight, hushed her with the desperate search of his mouth.

Everything seemed to impede Clifford's hands. He flung her shoes to the floor as he kissed her, ruined her pantyhose with a single jerk. He cursed his belt buckle, and his zipper which refused to surrender quickly enough.

"Clifford!" she gasped. "This house is full of people!"

"Kiss me quickly then."

That they were completely dressed didn't matter, nor the dozens of guests only yards beyond them and a couple of walls. There was nothing to do with the explosion of flames but to bury them deeply, and with such driving strength that Victoria flung her arms about his neck. She clung to his mouth, not daring to let go until her whimpering cries subsided like the calming of a stormy wind.

"Victoria? Are you in there?"

Stephanie's knock sounded unbelievably at the door.

Clifford heaved himself to an elbow, flushed, grappling with his breath. He smiled at Victoria's drugged and dreamy state. "Yes, Stephanie," he called. "What is it?"

For a tense moment no reply came from the other side of the door. Hastening, they both swung their legs off the sofa and adjusted their clothing. Clifford smoothed his hair and searched impatiently for his shoes. Victoria wasn't so easily repaired. Her tell-tale items went skidding beneath the furniture. Rising, putting on his shoes as he walked toward the door, Clifford swept it open and glared at the woman in silence.

"Ah yes, well," she finally choked out. "I'm afraid there's a small emergency in the kitchen, Mr. Pennington." She refused to meet his eyes.

"Oh?"

"Uh, yes . . . the oven. The thermostat is broken again. It couldn't have picked a worse time, could it?"

Uncertain if Stephanie unwittingly referred to the party or his state of disrepair, he straightened his tie without the slightest flicker of remorse.

"Darling?" Clifford drew Victoria a questioning glance as she attempted to slip her bare feet into her slings with a minimum of flurry. If Stephanie noticed anything from the corridor, she was much too tactful to allow it to show.

Victoria's hands lifted to her hair. "Come in, Steph."

"No! I mean, that's all right. I really have to get right back. Mamie's in a state and swears if Bud touches the oven the whole kitchen will explode."

"Tell Mamie I'll be right there," Clifford advised with a sly smile as he carefully closed the door in her face.

"I'm coming with you," Victoria said, her words garbled as she bent over her dressing table and reapplied her lipstick.

Clifford peered over the top of her head. "I can handle it," he said absently, then caught sight of the nape of her neck, so creamy and inviting. He stooped to plant a kiss behind her ear.

Straightening, Victoria turned in his arms. "I know you can, but this old place is a habit."

As he stood still, letting her fingers trail along the tendrils of hair on his collar, he thought how incredibly happy he was. So much lay beyond them: new, exciting things, old established ceremonies and traditions.

"You once said that Brayntree was all you ever wanted," he reminded her. He let her lean far back in the circle of his arms.

Her eyes danced with sated contentment. "Ah yes, but that was then. Now . . ."

"Go on."

Her lips curled, and she fluttered her fingers. "Now I want a diamond wedding ring. And I want a new car, Clifford. I just can't drive that jeep while I'm pregnant. And I'm positive we'll have to install a new oven for Mamie. Of course, there's still the plumbing in this place. Wretched stuff."

He clamped his finger over her mouth. "Hush. A diamond wedding ring, yes. And a new car, maybe. As for everything else, you'll just have to be patient."

Taking his arm, she smirked deliciously as they gave themselves one last satisfied inspection. "Patience was never my strongest virtue, Clifford Pennington."

Pulling the door shut behind them, Clifford peered down the long corridor to the bustle of thirty-five teenage female students and one Stephanie Morris. He sighed a little at the prospects of being just one man at their mercy. It would take a very strong hand.

Victoria didn't realize she was smiling. It would all work out; she knew it—the small tempest with Devon, Faith's adjustment, their own marriage, their daughter.

"It will be a girl," she said with absolute confidence.

Clifford peered down at her head, his eyes misting. "Really?"

"Yes." She continued walking without looking at him. "What I said before, about Brayntree being all I ever wanted. That wasn't true."

Clifford's step hesitated, but he said nothing.

"All I really want is you."

The copper highlights in her hair were never the same twice, he thought insanely and let her words flow through him like mellow wine. Then he grinned. "I guess that just got you the new car, lady," he said.

If you enjoyed this book...

..you will enjoy a Special Edition Book Club membership even more.

t will bring you each new title, as soon as it is published every month, delivered right to your door.

15-Day Free Trial Offer

We will send you 6 new Silhouette Special Editions to keep for 15 days absolutely free! If you decide not to keep them. send them back to us, you pay nothing. But if you enjoy them as much as we think you will, keep them and pay the nvoice enclosed with your trial shipment. You will then automatically become a member of the Special Edition Book Club and receive 6 more romances every month. There is no minimum number of books to buy and you can cancel at any time.

MORE ROMANCE FOR
A SPECIAL WAY TO RELAX

$1.95 each

1 ☐ TERMS OF SURRENDER Dailey

2 ☐ INTIMATE STRANGERS Hastings

3 ☐ MEXICAN RHAPSODY Dixon

4 ☐ VALAQUEZ BRIDE Vitek

5 ☐ PARADISE POSTPONED Converse

6 ☐ SEARCH FOR A NEW DAWN Douglass

7 ☐ SILVER MIST Stanford

8 ☐ KEYS TO DANIEL'S HOUSE Halston

9 ☐ ALL OUR TOMORROWS Baxter

10 ☐ TEXAS ROSE Thiels

11 ☐ LOVE IS SURRENDER Thornton

12 ☐ NEVER GIVE YOUR HEART Sinclair

13 ☐ BITTER VICTORY Beckman

14 ☐ EYE OF THE HURRICANE Keene

15 ☐ DANGEROUS MAGIC James

16 ☐ MAYAN MOON Carr

17 ☐ SO MANY TOMORROWS John

18 ☐ A WOMAN'S PLACE Hamilton

19 ☐ DECEMBER'S WINE Shaw

20 ☐ NORTHERN LIGHTS Musgrave

21 ☐ ROUGH DIAMOND Hastings

22 ☐ ALL THAT GLITTERS Howard

23 ☐ LOVE'S GOLDEN SHADOW Charles

24 ☐ GAMBLE OF DESIRE Dixon

25 ☐ TEARS AND RED ROSES Hardy

26 ☐ A FLIGHT OF SWALLOWS Scott

27 ☐ A MAN WITH DOUBTS Wisdom

28 ☐ THE FLAMING TREE Ripy

29 ☐ YEARNING OF ANGELS Bergen

30 ☐ BRIDE IN BARBADOS Stephens

31 ☐ TEARS OF YESTERDAY Baxter

32 ☐ A TIME TO LOVE Douglass

33 ☐ HEATHER'S SONG Palmer

34 ☐ MIXED BLESSING Sinclair

35 ☐ STORMY CHALLENGE James

36 ☐ FOXFIRE LIGHT Dailey

Silhouette Special Edition

MORE ROMANCE FOR
A SPECIAL WAY TO RELAX

**LOOK FOR *THE HEART'S VICTORY*
BY NORA ROBERTS AVAILABLE IN NOVEMBER
AND *TENDER DECEPTION* BY PATTI BECKMAN
IN DECEMBER.**

Silhouette Desire
15-Day Trial Offer
A new romance series that explores contemporary relationships in exciting detail

Six Silhouette Desire romances, free for 15 days! We'll send you six new Silhouette Desire romances to look over for 15 days, absolutely free! If you decide not to keep the books, return them and owe nothing.

Six books a month, free home delivery. If you like Silhouette Desire romances as much as we think you will, keep them and return your payment with the invoice. Then we will send you six new books every month to preview, just as soon as they are published. You pay only for the books you decide to keep, and you never pay postage and handling.

READERS' COMMENTS ON SILHOUETTE SPECIAL EDITIONS:

"I just finished reading the first six Silhouette Special Edition Books and I had to take the opportunity to write you and tell you how much I enjoyed them. I enjoyed all the authors in this series. Best wishes on your Silhouette Special Editions line and many thanks."

—B.H.*, Jackson, OH

"The Special Editions are really special and I enjoyed them very much! I am looking forward to next month's books."

—R.M.W.*, Melbourne, FL

"I've just finished reading four of your first six Special Editions and I enjoyed them very much. I like the more sensual detail and longer stories. I will look forward each month to your new Special Editions."

—L.S.*, Visalia, CA

"Silhouette Special Editions are — 1.) Superb! 2.) Great! 3.) Delicious! 4.) Fantastic! . . . Did I leave anything out? These are books that an adult woman can read . . . I love them!"

—H.C.*, Monterey Park, CA

* names available on request